MACROECONOMICS and the
CANADIAN ECONOMY

MACROECONOMICS AND THE CANADIAN ECONOMY

PAUL PHILLIPS

Department of Economics
University of Manitoba

JAMES SELDON

Department of Economics
University of Manitoba

D.C.HEATH   CANADA   LIMITED   Toronto

EDITORIAL
Malcolm Lester Editorial Associates
DESIGN/TYPESETTING/ILLUSTRATIONS
Cerebrus Productions Incorporated

Printed in Canada.

ISBN 0-669-80606-4

Preface

This book is designed as an introduction to macroeconomics at the first year university level. It is primarily intended for principles courses, although it carries the theoretical analysis beyond what is usually taught at this level by including a fairly full presentation of the Hicks-Hansen and Mundell formulations of Keynesian theory. This makes it suitable for one semester courses in macroeconomics, for select classes, for supplemental use in money and banking and intermediate theory courses, for those classes where some introduction to economics has already been taken, as well as for the standard type introductory course. On the other hand, for those teachers who hesitate to lead their students into such deep waters, the appendices to Chapter 6 (the Hicks-Hansen model) and to Chapter 8 (the Mundell model) may easily be ommitted without interrupting the overall presentation.

Three themes run through this book and receive probably more stress than is general in most introductory texts. First is the close integration between the theory of aggregate behaviour and microeconomics. Second, there is considerable attention paid to the international sector. And third, the particular problems and circumstances of the Canadian economy, its dependence on the international sector, its regional disparities and structures, its specific institutions, are emphasized, particularly in the last chapter. As a result, it is hoped that the student will gain a better understanding of the application of macro principles within the Canadian setting.

The presentation is deliberately concise because the authors feel that extended exposition can often intimidate and confuse the student before the basic theorems are developed. Also, there are a host of other textual materials readily available to students to supplement this presentation should the need arise.

We are deeply indebted to our students who acted as guinea pigs and to our colleagues for their encouragement and suggestions for improvements. However, as always, deficiencies and errors are the shared responsibility only of the authors.

The Plan of the Book

Our basic plan is to begin with the relatively easy concepts involved in accounting for incomes and expenditures in the Canadian economy (Chapter 2). These flows of income and expenditure will then be placed within a simplified "model" of the economy, a model based on the analysis of the noted British economist John Maynard Keynes. With each subsequent chapter, the model will be elaborated with the introduction first, of the government sector and its tax and expenditure (fiscal) policies; second, of the role of money and the government's or central bank's control over money supply and interest rates (monetary policy); and third, of the international sector and the effects of international trade and monetary capital movements on our level of income and employment. We shall then be in a better position to compare (and, we hope, to reconcile) the macroeconomic approach to economic analysis with the microeconomic.

The proof of our theoretical pudding, of course, is in the eating. While we introduce relevant statistical and institutional material throughout, the real test of our model is its applicability to the total Canadian economy. Our work is thus "tested" in the final chapter, where we deal with a selected list of current Canadian economic problems. In theory or in its application, this book is not in any sense an exhaustive study. It is an introduction — to whet the appetite of those who really wish to understand the workings of our economy but, at the same time, to cool the ardour of those who might expect to find easy answers to all our problems.

Introduction to the Student

This book may at first seem rather strange to students who have looked at other "Principles" texts — for one thing, it is *not* 1059 pages in length; for another, it is *not* designed to tell you "everything you always wanted to know about macroeconomics but were afraid to ask"; and for another, it may at first glance seem to be rather mathematical for a first introduction to economics.

What the book *is* intended to be is a clear (we hope), concise (we are sure) view of macroeconomics, a treatment which clears away some of the trees so that we can begin to see the forest. Furthermore, while it is meant as an introduction to economics, we hope that you will find it a useful summary of basic macroeconomic theory, and that it will be of value in reviewing for future macroeconomics courses.

"The trees" in this case refer to the wide range of institutions and events which clutter up any attempt to see how an economic system "really" works.

We make use of a large number of graphs throughout the book for a very specific reason, not to make the approach a "mathematical" one, but simply to save space and effort for both the reader and the writers! The words needed to replace the graphs would make the discussion a rather lengthy one, and, believe it or not, much more difficult. If you think that you will have trouble working with the graphical treatment, the short appendix on graphs at the end of the book should help clear up your problems.

Our graphs are only pictures, and a picture is indeed worth a thousand words!

The text follows a pattern of beginning with very simple diagrams, carefully plotting the data shown in accompanying tables; then gradually doing away with the tables; and finally dispensing with precise scales on the axes.

This progression does not really mean that we are becoming less and less accurate as we go along, just that we do not want to be tied to a specific set of numbers in discussing our "models" of the economy's behaviour.

If a theory is "good", it is because it describes in a simplified way, the working of the real world. If it doesn't give us good predictions about the real world, then it's time to build a better one.

As an example of common ground, all economics whether capitalist, communist, socialist, or mixed must answer the basic questions of what to produce, how to produce those goods, and for whom to produce. It is simply that the exact ways in which these matters are decided differ.

The first nine chapters have been kept at a more or less theoretical level, providing a "core" approach to macro-economic theory, and leaving out most of the descriptive material which fills up principles books. To remind you — and us — that the subject matter of economics cannot be neatly divided up into "theory" and "reality" packages, we introduce descriptive material where it is needed to develop the theory, and where it serves to show how the theory can be of use to us in simplifying the workings of a real-world economy. We hope that Chapter 10, which deals with a number of Canadian economic problems, will convince you that the theory is there to be *used*, not to be put in a glass case and admired.

The marginal notes are intended to help you in two ways. First, they provide a number of examples and elaborations of the accompanying textual discussion. Second, they refer to other sources of information and description on the same subject, to allow you to see just how other writers deal with the same topic and to help you to fill in some of the detail we have deliberately omitted. We urge you, if our explanation seems unclear or too brief, to consult these alternative sources for clarification or amplification. In this way you should get much more from your studies.

Our discussion *does* concentrate on what can broadly be termed "capitalist" economies, but while the institutions in a "mixed" or "socialist" economy may be quite different, societies in general face the same types of economic issues we discuss.

In short, our main goal is to introduce you to the basic analytic tools which go into the economist's tool box, and more, to persuade you to try using them yourself!

Table of Contents

1

The Basic Setting

The Problem

Our economic life has many perspectives, many facets. The student of economics sometimes directs his magnifying glass at one facet of the economy, sometimes at another. The most important division that is customarily made in economic theory is between *microeconomics* and *macroeconomics*. As one might suspect, microeconomics deals with small parts of the economy, and macroeconomics with the total activity of the economy or, as it is sometimes called, *aggregate* economics.

It is easier to understand this distinction through a diagram of the flows of goods, services, and factors of production (land, labour and capital) and the counterflows of money payments.

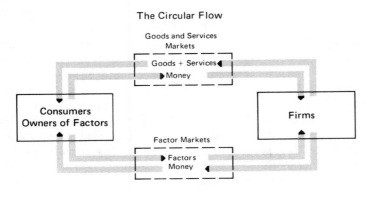

FIGURE 1-1

Microeconomics goes behind the goods and services markets, behind the factor markets, to the behaviour of individual consumers, owners of factors, firms, industries — and sees their behaviour in isolation, each part temporarily independent of the other. Macroeconomics, on the other hand, is a study of the total economic activity, the aggregation of all the decisions, cast not in terms of the isolated economic decisions, but in terms of the broad aggregates of production, consumption and income flows. It deals with total levels of income, employment, saving, investment, prices, consumption — the size of and fluctuations in the circular flow of income pictured above.

For this reason, macroeconomics has emerged centre stage, not only in the theoretical studies of the economist, but also in the pages of the daily newspapers, in Parliament and the provincial legislatures, and in the day to day concerns of all our population. An understanding is important, therefore, not only as a basis for deeper study, but for an appreciation of the real world we live in.

Let us consider in a little more detail the circular flow diagram pictured above. This is a very simplified picture of the economy as it omits such important parts as the government sector and the foreign trade sector, in addition to some important flows such as savings and investment. However, while these are very important in real life, for our purposes in introducing the student to the study of macroeconomics, they only complicate the basic processes of the economy.

Our diagram shows the two major elements in our economy: the firms which combine the factors (land, labour and capital) bought from the consumers (everyone in the economy) to produce goods and services for the market; and the consumers who supply these factors to firms and who purchase the goods and services the firms put on the market. Thus, it should be clear that the income of firms is the expenditure of consumers and that the income of consumers is the expenditure of firms on factors. One can see why it is called the circular flow, as income circulates from firms to consumers and back to firms.

Let us be sure that we know what factors are. Firms hire labour for wages, land for rent, and capital (machinery and buildings used in the production of other goods) for interest.* Any excess profits of firms over and above factor payments are paid out as income to the owners of the firms. Therefore, the income of consumers (the payments of firms) comprises wages, rents, interest and profits. The

_____

*Actually, firms usually buy the capital with money borrowed either from shareholders or lending institutions. The cost of acquiring the capital, therefore, is the interest paid on the money borrowed to finance that capital.

concern of macroeconomics is the determination of the total flows of expenditure and income.

Micro and Macroeconomics

What is the relationship between micro and macroeconomics? We have talked above about the expenditures of consumers on goods and services and of firms on factors. In macroeconomics, these are total or aggregate expenditures, the sum of all the expenditures in each and every specific market. In microeconomics, we are concerned with the determination of prices, quantities and expenditures in the specific markets, holding everything else in the economy constant. This allows us to study in detail the process in these specific markets independent of changes in other facets of the economy. In simple terms, we look at the supply of and the demand for a good or a factor in a given market, and at the equilibrium price and quantity (that price and quantity where there is no market pressure to change).

In reality, however, it is largely impossible to isolate a specific market. For instance, how can we determine the level of demand for labour in the manufacture of cars until we know the demand for cars. But can we know the demand for cars until we know (among other things) the incomes of wage earners employed in the manufacture of cars? In some cases these cross effects will be small; in others, large. In theory, we can solve this problem through "general equilibrium analysis", which means that we bring all our specific markets to equilibrium simultaneously. In practice, this is a horrendous problem and hence we use a different technique, the summing up of supply and demand into one aggregate supply and one aggregate demand function for the whole economy. Thus, we can look at the economy from a different perspective, the perspective of macroeconomics.*

The Framework

The kind of economy we are dealing with is the modern capitalist system such as exists in North America. This is not to say that "capitalist system" has a specific meaning and that macroeconomic analysis can only be applied to such a specific system. There are many types and degrees of capitalism. The common denominator is that the majority of micro decisions are taken by firms owned privately and the distribution of income is determined largely by

*The whole question of the relationship between micro and macroeconomics is pursued in more depth in Chapter 9.

Wage and price controls have occasionally been used in an attempt to regulate aggregate economic activity (usually in a fight against inflation), but since they tend to be relatively inflexible as far as micro markets are concerned, they are only useful as a short-term weapon. Some of the issues raised by wage and price controls are discussed in Chapter 10.

the ownership of factors. As we shall see, the reality in Canada is that a significant part of economic decision making in our economy, around a third, is done by public bodies, and that governments are considerably involved in redistributing incomes.

Nor is there any theoretical reason why, in our circular flow concept, the firms could not be 100 per cent publicly owned. The same flows of expenditure and incomes must occur. The major difference results from the fact that in a centrally planned economy, the decisions determining aggregate expenditure and aggregate incomes may be controlled by a central plan rather than by being left to the individual consumers and producers. The results of two such systems can differ markedly.

Our concern in this book, therefore, is with the system operating in Canada. While such theorizing may be broadly applicable to all similar economies, outside of North America as well as within, there are certain institutions that are particular to each country. In Canada, we have a particular banking and monetary system, a federal governmental apparatus, a distinctly regional economy, a largely open economy (that is, depending significantly on the international sector), and in general a specific set of political, legal, social and economic institutions which must be considered and understood, before we can comprehend the working of the system as a whole. In building up our model, therefore, we shall put these institutions in place.

2

The Framework of Macroeconomic Analysis: The National Accounts

Introduction

As early as the seventeenth century, people had become concerned with measuring the output of national economies. The pioneering effort was made by an Englishman, Gregory King, when he published his *Social Accounts of England and Wales for 1688*. Surprisingly, however, Canada did not develop a consistent series measuring national output and income and their components until the years between the First and Second World Wars. The series now used begins in 1926 and is called *National Accounts — Income and Expenditure*. Before going into Canada's national accounts, it is necessary to show why they are important to our study of macroeconomics.

Earlier, macroeconomics was defined as the study of the aggregate flows of income and expenditure and the level of employment and prices in the whole economy and of what determines their level and composition. The national accounts give us the measure we need for such a study. They provide not only information on welfare standards within the economy such as income per capita, but also the necessary statistics for analysing the performance of the economy in the past, the present and the future. Also, as one economist has put it, they provide the conceptual building blocks for erecting the theory of income determination.

Although the Canadian statistics were not collected until this rather recent date, the Dominion Bureau of Statistics work served as a model for a number of other countries.

The National Accounts and the Circular Flow

To understand the national accounts, we may find it useful to refer to an elaborated circular flow diagram (Figure 2-1). Remember, what we are trying to account for is the total flow of income and expenditure in the economy.

For each transaction that takes place, there is a counter flow of money. Since money is the only common denominator in all exchanges, we measure the money flows rather than the flow of goods, services and factors directly.

The key measure in the national accounts is the *Gross National Product* (GNP) — the value of the total output of the economy. It can be calculated in three ways: (1) summing the total of all expenditures on Canadian goods and services (referred to as *Gross National Expenditure at Market Prices* or GNE); (2) summing the value added by firms at each stage of production from raw materials to the final sale (a method which is no longer used in Canada); and (3) summing the incomes paid out to the factors of production (wages, interest, rent and profits, which comprises *Net National Income at Factor Cost* — NNI), adding what is paid by the firms directly to the government before distributing income to factors (Indirect Taxes), and what is put aside by firms to cover depreciation or the "using up" of capital assets (*Capital Consumption Allowances*).

Simplified Circular Flow of Income in an Open Economy

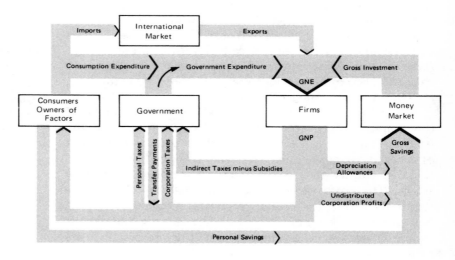

FIGURE 2-1

That the two measures must be the same, except for minor statistical errors, should be apparent. In any case, it can be illustrated by the following balance sheet of revenues and payments of the combined business sector of the economy.

6

Revenues	*Payments*
1. Sales of goods and services to the final consumer	1. Payments to the factors of production
	(a) wages for labour
2. Sales of capital goods to firms for use in production (capital investment)	(b) interest for investment capital
	(c) rent for land
	(d) profits
3. Sales of goods to firms for the building up of inventories	2. Payments directly to the government as indirect taxes
4. Sales of goods and services to the government	3. Payments to a savings fund to cover the depreciation of capital (Capital Consumption Allowances)
5. Sales of goods and services to foreigners	

It should be noted that sales of goods to firms for the building up of inventories can be positive or negative. This is because we are really measuring net sales to firms for inventories and firms may be selling to final markets goods produced in a previous period and stored as inventories without replacing them.

In this way we can see that the revenue of firms, (private or public firms since government operated corporations are treated exactly the same as private firms) is all disbursed in the form of payments. Any residual in revenue after payments to factors (land, labour and capital), direct payments to government as indirect taxes, and appropriations for capital depreciation is, by definition, profit payments. Hence, the entire revenue of the business sector is exhausted.

We have defined the value of total payments as the *Gross National Product*. It is called "gross" because it does not make any allowance for capital goods which are used up in the production process. If we do not replace these capital goods, if we consume all our annual output, our accumulated wealth of capital goods would eventually all be used up. This is why some current output must be put aside to compensate for depreciation. This is the capital consumption or depreciation allowance.

GNP minus *Depreciation Allowances* (Dep) can be defined as *Net National Product* (NNP), a measure not normally used in Canada. In general, it measures the net value of the supply of goods and services in the economy in a given year.

Total Gross National Product figures are of little use in international comparisons. Even GNP per capita figures are debatable measures for comparing international welfare standards because of statistical problems, different modes of life and different degrees of monetization of markets. For what they are worth, however, here are some comparative values for selected developed and under-developed countries.

Country	GNP/capita, 1968
	(in U.S. dollars)
Canada	*2,877*
United States	*4,120*
Sweden	*3,130*
France	*2,399*
United Kingdom	*2,071*
Japan	*1,283*
Mexico	*546*
Ghana	*215*
Pakistan	*116*
India	*86*

Source: *Agency for International Development*

Firms make other payments before distributing their revenues to the public. The first of these is the payment of indirect taxes directly to the government. These taxes include primarily sales taxes, property taxes and customs and excise taxes, and must be paid before any income is distributed. At the same time, the government gives certain subsidies and grants to some businesses. These are, in effect, negative taxes. When these subsidies are subtracted from total indirect taxes paid in to the government, we arrive at *Net Indirect Taxes* (T_{in}).

The remainder is then paid out to factors. This comprises the actual income of the population — paid out as wages, interest, rent and profits — or *Net National Income* (NNI). Table 2-1 shows how this income is then distributed. Businesses receive profits, interest and rent payments, but only some of this income is distributed to shareholders or other owners. Part must be paid as corporation income taxes (T_b). Also some business income is usually put aside as business savings (S_b) for current or future use.

What is left of the income flow, plus government transfer payments to persons (tp — which includes such transfers as family allowances, unemployment insurance, old age pensions and all such similar benefits), is distributed as income to persons — or *Personal Income* (PI). This represents the actual income that is passed into the hands of the general population. Not all, however, is available for use by these people. *Personal Taxes* (T_p) — mainly income taxes — are deducted, leaving what is actually available for disposal by the general population, or *Personal Disposable Income* (DI). It is either spent for consumption (C) or saved (S_p). This exhausts the income flow. In tabular form we can show the lower flow thus:

TABLE 2-1

Gross National Product	GNP
subtract: Depreciation for capital consumption allowances	$-$ Dep
Net National Product	NNP
subtract: Indirect taxes minus subsidies	$- T_{in}$
Net National Income	NNI
subtract: Business savings (undistributed corporation profits)	$- S_b$
Business taxes	$- T_b$
add: Transfer payments	$+$ tp
Personal Income	PI
subtract: Personal taxes	$- T_p$
Personal Disposable Income	DI
subtract: Personal savings	$- S_p$
Consumption	C

8

We can see, then, that the income flow is disposed of in three ways:

1. *Taxes* — includes net indirect taxes, business taxes, and personal taxes (minus transfer payments which can be considered as negative taxes), or

$$T = T_{in} + T_b + T_p - tp$$

2. *Gross Savings* — includes actual savings set aside to cover depreciation (capital consumption allowances), business savings (undistributed corporation profits), and personal saving, or

$$S_{gross} = Dep + S_b + S_p$$

3. *Consumption* = C

Hence we see that

$$GNP \equiv C + S_{gross} + T$$

If we consider only the net flow of income to exclude the allowance for depreciation then:

$$NNP \equiv C + S + T \text{ (where S is net saving = } S_b + S_p)$$

The Expenditure Side

Let us now return to our balance sheet to review the components that comprise the aggregate revenue of the business sector. Their total, of course, must match the payments out of the business sector that we have just analyzed.

First, goods and services are sold directly to final consumers. If these consumers bought nothing from foreign countries, then these sales to consumers would exactly equal consumption out of disposable income — that is, C (as above). However, Canadians do purchase goods imported from other countries. Therefore, their purchases of goods and services from the Canadian business sector is C minus consumption of imports or $(C - M_c)$, where M_c is the value of imported consumption goods. This is the first component of expenditure on Canadian output.

Second, goods are sold by businesses to other businesses and also to themselves. These are capital goods to be used in the production of other goods and services. This we call *Capital Investment*. We must include only those goods that are never resold in another form. We do not include, for example, shoe leather that is sold by a tanner to a shoe manufacturer because that is resold as shoes to the final

It is often assumed when we refer to the fiscal powers of government, that the Canadian (federal) government is the main taxing and spending body. In fact, in 1970 the federal government accounted for 51 per cent of all tax collections but only 40 per cent of total government expenditures. For the provinces the comparable figures were 34 per cent of taxes and 27 per cent of expenditures. Local and hospital governments account for the remainder, 15 per cent of tax revenues and 33 per cent of expenditures.

consumer and is already counted in consumption. But firms buy capital goods for two reasons: (1) to replace used up or depreciated capital (our depreciation, *Dep*) and (2) to add new capital goods to their stock. Thus, we have depreciation plus net capital investment, comprising *Gross Capital Investment*.

Third, goods are sold by businesses to other firms and very often to themselves to build up their inventories or stocks of goods to be sold at a future date. Sometimes businesses plan to build up these stocks — sometimes the sales they expect don't materialize and the stocks rise unexpectedly. In either case, they are known as *Inventory Investment*. It should be remembered that inventories don't always go up. Almost as often they go down, which means that firms are selling more than they are producing. This then is *Inventory Disinvestment* or a *Negative Inventory Investment*.

If we take all forms of investment together we get *Gross Investment*.

$$I_{gross} = \text{Dep} + \text{Net Capital Investment} + \text{Net Inventory Investment}$$

If we exclude depreciation, we get *Net Investment* (I).

Again, not all investment goods (of any sort) are purchased from Canadian firms. Some are imported. Therefore, the total sale of investment goods by Canadian business is *Gross Investment* minus *Imported Investment* goods (M_I), or $I_{gross} - M_I$.

Fourth, the government buys goods and services from Canadian business and foreigners. The *Net Government Expenditure* on Canadian output is, therefore, *Government Expenditure* (G) minus *Government Purchased Imports* (M_G), or $G - M_G$.

Fifth, foreigners buy goods from Canadian firms. These are our *Exports* (X).

We can then sum up the total expenditures on the output of the Canadian economy — which is called *Gross National Expenditure* (GNE).

$$\text{GNE} \equiv (C - M_C) + (I_{gross} - M_I) + (G - M_G) + X$$

Finally, we can add all the imports together to make things much simpler.

$$\text{GNE} \equiv C + I_{gross} + G + (X - M)$$

$$(\text{where } M = M_C + M_I + M_G)$$

As with our income analysis we can subtract depreciation to give us what might be called *Net National Expenditure* or *Net National Product*.

$$NNP \equiv C + I + G + (X - M)$$

$$\text{(where } I = I_{gross} - Dep)$$

We are thus left with two identity equations which sum up the total disbursements of the expenditure (GNP).

Since there are two ways of measuring the same flow of income and expenditure, they must in the end be the same (except for small errors of measurement).

$$GNE \equiv GNP$$

$$\text{Therefore, } C + I_{gross} + G + (X - M) \equiv C + S_{gross} + T$$

or subtracting depreciation from both sides:

$$C + I + G + (X - M) \equiv C + S + T$$

$$\text{(where I and S are net of depreciation)}$$

Problems of Measurement in the Canadian Statistics

In theory, as can be seen, the collection and measurement of national income and expenditure and their components appear straightforward. In fact, it is not quite so easy. For example, how do you decide what proportion of the income of farmers and small unincorporated businesses is wages, interest, rent or profits? As you can see from Table 2-2, we don't try, Also, since prices are not usually constant from year to year, the value of inventories changes even when there is no inventory investment or disinvestment. Therefore, we have to introduce what is called the *Inventory Valuation Adjustment.*

A major problem in any national accounting is what to do with goods and services that are not evaluated in the market. For example, if you rent a house, your transaction is measured and included in the market. However, if you own your own house, you in effect are paying rent to yourself and of course this is not recorded in the market. We must, therefore, impute or estimate the value of this imputed rent for inclusion in our statistics.

On the other hand, housewives' work in the home, producing services which are not evaluated in the market, is not included in national income or expenditure. Yet, if these same women go out and do the same work in other peoples' homes for pay, it is included. No one has yet devised a perfect way of handling this statistical problem.

Within the broad statistical categories, we can break our

Some excellent work has been done in many countries to produce consistent series of economic statistics going back for many years. In Canada, the most comprehensive work is Canadian Historical Statistics, *edited by M. C. Urquhart and K. A. H. Buckley, Macmillan Co., Toronto, 1965. The comparable United States reference is* Historical Statistics of the United States, Colonial Times to 1957, *issued by the U.S. Bureau of the Census, Washington D.C., 1960.*

If the feminists win their battle to have housewives paid regular salaries, we will observe a sharp increase (perhaps as much as 25%) in GNP figures, but of course there will be no real change in the economy's production of goods and services when all resources are fully employed.

11

accounts down into finer and finer divisions for specific purposes.* However, for economic analysis, the basic breakdown in Table 2-2 is our most useful framework of aggregate economic activity.

TABLE 2-2

National Accounts — 1970
(Millions of Dollars)

Expenditure			*Income*	
Personal Expenditure on Consumer Goods & Services (C)		48,995	Wages and Salaries	47,043
			Military Pay and Allowances	906
Gross Fixed Capital Formation by Business	14,709		Interest and Miscellaneous Investment Income	3,614
Physical Change in Inventories	135		Unincorporated Business Income	4,551
			Farm Income	1,369
Total Investment (I_{gross})		14,844	Net Corporation Profits before Taxes*	6,458
			Inventory Valuation Adjustment	− 171
Government Expenditure on Goods & Services (G)		19,041	Net National Income at Factor Cost	63,770
Exports of Goods & Services (X)		20,969	Indirect Taxes (net)	11,251
Imports of Goods & Services (M)		−19,833	Capital Consumption Allowances	9,898
Residual Error of Estimate		452	Residual Error of Estimate	− 451
			Gross National Product at Market Prices	84,468
GNE at Market Prices		84,468		

*(excluding dividends paid to non-residents)

Personal Sector

Savings (S_p)		3,975
Taxes	12,505	
— Transfer Payments	6,804	
Net Taxes (T_p)		5,701

Business Sector

Undistributed Profits (S_b)	2,434
Taxes (T_b)	2,830

Source: Statistics Canada, *Canadian Statistical Review,* 1971.

*One such category, for instance, is *Gross Domestic Product*. Whereas GNP is a measure of the income earned by residents of Canada, GDP is a measure of income originating in Canada and can be calculated by subtracting from GNP indirect taxes less subsidies and payments to Canadian residents from foreign countries and adding payments from Canada to foreigners.

Summary

1.   The national accounts are a comprehensive statistical record of Canada's income and expenditure and their components. The two major series are the Gross National Product, calculated by summing the total incomes of all factors, and the Gross National Expenditure, calculated from the total expenditures on goods and services by all sectors of the economy.

2.   Gross National Product is composed of depreciation, taxes, savings and consumption ($GNP \equiv Dep + C + S + T$).

3.   Gross National Expenditure is composed of gross investment (depreciation plus net investment), consumption, government expenditure and net foreign expenditure on Canadian goods (exports minus imports). ($GNE \equiv C + I_{gross} + G + (X - M)$).

Questions for Discussion

1.   Should the value of housewives' services be included in the national accounts? If so, how would you evaluate these services?

2.   Should the costs of pollution be subtracted from the gross national product? Why or why not?

3.   A firm producing curling brooms pays the following bills for a month's operation. Sale of the brooms brings $1,200.

Item	$
Straw	500
Electricity	10
Rent	100
Wood for handles	75
Wages	400
Interest on machinery	15
Depreciation on machinery	10
Printing of labels	10
Shipping cost	30
Indirect (business) taxes	10

What is the value added (its contribution to GNP) of the firm? What is the firm's contribution to net national income?

4.   A retired politician appointed to the Canadian Senate is paid a salary. This is part of government expenditure. A retired civil servant is paid a pension. This is called a transfer payment. "Roses may have different names but they smell the same." Discuss.

3

The Determination of the Level
of Income and Employment:

The Basic Keynesian Model

In the previous chapter we showed how the flows of income and expenditure are measured and what they are composed of. We have not answered the more fundamental question — what determines what the flow of income and expenditure *is* in any given year?

We must first distinguish between economic growth and economic fluctuations. Economic growth is the increase in output over time which results from the increased use of factors and the increased productivity of factors due to technological improvement. Economic fluctuations represent the difference between what *could* be produced if all resources are fully employed and what actually *is* produced in the economy at a given point in time. (See Appendix Table 3-1 for levels of output and unemployment in Canada.) The difference is illustrated for a hypothetical economy in Figure 3-1. Potential output is shown by the line GG'. The increase in output over time is a measure of economic growth, with which we will not be dealing. Our concern will be with line FF' which shows that output does not always equal what potentially the economy could produce. The question is why.

The Economic Council of Canada has attempted to estimate the behaviour of potential and actual GNP for recent years. This estimate is reproduced here graphically.

Note: The potential output line is drawn heavily in this Chart to convey the impression that it is a rough calculation and that its value depends on both the method of calculation and the assumptions used.

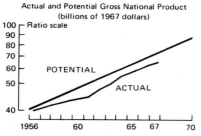

Actual and Potential Gross National Product
(billions of 1967 dollars)

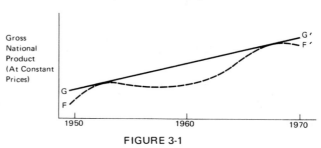

FIGURE 3-1

14

Concern with this problem by economists was largely the result of the great depression of the 1930s. People were starving and in abject poverty. Yet capital was lying idle, land was unused, and almost a quarter of the labour force was unable to find work. How could such unemployment exist when people were denied even the necessities? Since that time, economists and governments have become committed to preventing such a situation from happening again. At the same time, they are committed to preventing inflation, a general and persistent rise in prices that erodes the buying power of money — such as occurred in Germany in the 1920s where money earned one day had to be spent the same day before it had become almost worthless. The authorities are thus concerned with *stabilization* of the economy, but stabilization at a particular level of economic activity. The goals for the Canadian economy set forth by the Economic Council of Canada, for instance, include as two of its five primary goals (1) full employment and (2) reasonable price stability. Our concern, first, will be with the equilibrium between aggregate supply and aggregate demand, which determines the level of national economic activity; and second, with the question of whether this coincides with a position of unemployment, full employment without inflation, or full employment with inflation. Before we can deal with these matters, however, we must go back to the determination of aggregate supply and aggregate demand.

"although it has been claimed in later years by some economists, that from 1934 onwards, there was an upswing in world economy, I don't think that anybody in B.C. or Canada noticed it at the time, or at any time before the start of the Second World War. Right at that time, millions of people in the world were hungry and at the same time, thousands of tons of coffee were dumped into the sea off the mouth of the Amazon river; the U.S. government paid the farmers a small dole not to sow any crops; cotton and wheat were burned up; three million pigs were slaughtered and destroyed in the United States; fish which the people could not buy was thrown back into the sea; fruit was left to rot in the orchards. This was the depression . . ." (from Ronald Liversedge, Recollections of the On-To-Ottawa Trek, 1935 *p. 76-7).*

Aggregate Supply

We can define aggregate supply as the value of the total amount of final goods and services placed on the market. If, at the given level of prices, firm A puts $Q_1 P_1$ worth of goods on the market, firm B puts $Q_2 P_2$, firm C puts $Q_3 P_3$ etc., then the aggregate supply is:

$$AS = Q_1 P_1 + Q_2 P_2 + Q_3 P_3 + \ldots + Q_n P_n$$

(where Q equals the amount of goods produced by each firm and P the prices of which they are sold).

If we sum up the value of total production of final goods produced for the market, we get GNP or, as we shall normally use after subtracting depreciation, NNP at constant prices — the net addition to the flow of goods and services in any given period. Aggregate supply, therefore, may be defined as the same as real NNP providing that prices remain constant. At full employment, all productive resources are being put to their most efficient use, and it is impossible for the economy to produce any more goods and services. Therefore, if the value of aggregate supply is to increase any further, it can only come about through a rise in prices. This can be shown in Figure 3-2. Aggregate supply equals NNP at constant prices up to full employment. Since real output cannot increase beyond this point, prices must rise. This is represented by the vertical part of the supply line — a constant real NNP but a rising AS or a rising NNP if measured in money terms.

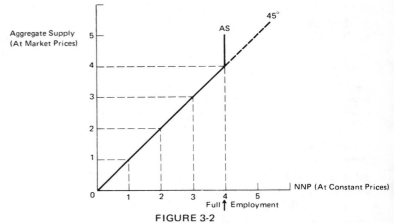

FIGURE 3-2

In this simplified model we shall assume that there is no government sector and no international sector. Therefore, NNP as we have defined it in the previous chapter equals the income of the factors; or NNP = C + S. This is true whether NNP is measured in constant prices (in which case we must also measure C and S in constant prices) or whether it is measured in market prices (in which case C and S are also measured in market prices). In order to pre-

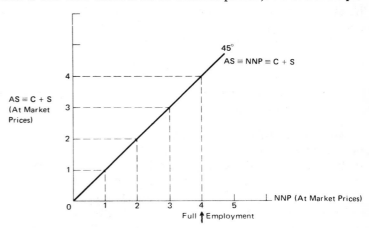

FIGURE 3-3

16

vent any confusion, we shall, from this point on, measure both NNP and AS in market prices. In this case, therefore, the value of AS is the value of goods and services put on the market, which is by definition equal to the incomes paid out by firms to the factors of production, or to the NNP at market prices, which in turn equals $C + S$. This is illustrated in Figure 3-3 where the $45°$ line indicates the points where AS as measured on the vertical axis is equivalent to the *money* NNP measured in the horizontal axis — or where $AS \equiv NNP \equiv C + S$.

Aggregate Demand

In our simplified model of the world, the total demand for goods and services must equal the demand by consumers plus the demand by firms for investment goods. This may be represented by:

$$AD = C + I_{intended}$$

(where $I_{intended}$ is intended or planned investment by firms).

It is necessary to go behind these components of aggregate demand to understand how they are affected by changes in the level of economic activity. We shall consider first the level of consumption demand.

The Consumption Function

Give a person an income and there are only two things he can do with it — spend it or save it. That is, he either consumes his income or he saves it, since we define saving as abstinence from consumption. You might ask: what if he uses part of his income to buy shares in a company, uses the money to set himself up in business, or buys some capital? In each case, he is still saving. But he is then lending his savings; in the first case, to a corporation which may then use it to finance investment; in the second and third cases, to himself for the financing of investment on his own behalf as a business. It should become obvious that the decision to spend or to save is necessarily the same decision. We will look at the choice from the point of view of the decision to spend.

It is useful to begin by considering the probable behaviour of an individual or a single family, Take, for instance, a worker in a factory earning normally an average wage. He probably spends ninety per cent or more of his current income, putting the remainder into pension savings, a savings account at a bank or credit union, and possibly paying into a union benefit fund. Let us say that during a slack period at the factory he is laid off, and his income is reduced to zero. His consumption, of course, would not fall to zero. Needless to say that if it did, there would soon be one less unemployed worker to worry about. He would finance his consumption out of past saving or, in other words, he would dissave, drawing from his savings account or his union unemployed benefit or possibly cashing in a life insurance policy with its accrued savings. Assume that he is rehired on a short time basis — say one day a week. His income rises, but it is likely that he will continue to dissave although at a slower rate. If we continue the argument, his consumption and savings sheet might look some-like that in Table 3-1:

TABLE 3-1

Annual Income	Consumption	Savings
$ 0	$3,000	$ −3,000
1,000	3,500	−2,500
2,000	4,000	−2,000
4,000	5,000	−1,000
6,000	6,000	0
7,000	6,500	500

The actual level of his consumption will depend on a lot of things — his real income, his personal attitudes and tastes, his family size, his wealth, his income over several years, etc., but in general, we can expect a behaviour similar to that pictured above as his income fluctuates.

It is always hazardous to generalize from the behaviour of a single individual to that of an entire economy. Yet, there are good reasons for believing that people in aggregate would behave in a manner similar to that of our sample citizen. Economists have tried to show this in two ways, by *time series* analysis and by *cross sectional* analysis.* Time series data indicates that aggregate consumption has risen in much the same way as illustrated in our example as personal disposable income has grown over a number of years. Figures 3-4 and 3-5 show the value of consumption in Canada compared with the level of output for the period since 1926. Note that the ratio of consumption to GNP has remained fairly steady since the Second World War. Cross sectional data indicates that consumption is greater among families with higher incomes than it is among similar types of families with smaller incomes. However, neither of these methods is entirely satisfactory, because they still do not show what a parti-

For a clear and concise introduction to the concept of the consumption function, see James Tobin's article, "Consumption Function", in the International Encyclopedia of the Social Sciences, *ed. D. L. Sills, pp. 358-368, Crowell Collier and McMillan Inc., 1968.*

*Time series data records levels of income and consumption over-time — for example, in annual figures for the Canadian economy. Cross-sectional data records consumption and income levels for different sectors of the economy at a particular point in time.

cular family or group of families will do if their income is varied at any specific time.

Consumption and Gross National Product, 1926-1970

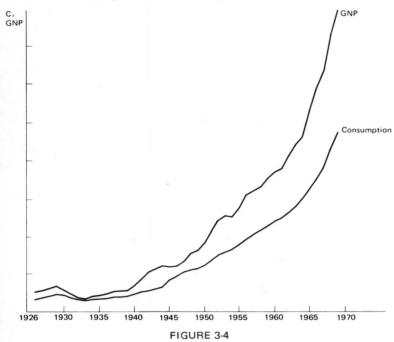

FIGURE 3-4

FIGURE 3-5

19

Given such behaviour, the demand for consumption goods by the whole of society will follow the pattern of being lowest where national income approaches zero, and increasing as national income increases. That is, we say that aggregate consumption demand is a function of (depends upon) national income. The relationships between national income, consumption and savings are shown in Table 3-2, and they are illustrated in Figure 3-6, which makes use of the dollar values set out in the table. Remember, NNP is identically equal to C + S (or aggregate supply). This is represented by the 45° line from the origin, which depicts all points where NNP, measured on the X-axis, is equal to C + S, or aggregate supply, measured on the Y-axis.

TABLE 3-2

NNP	C	S
	(millions of dollars)	
0	1200	—1200
2000	2800	— 800
4000	4400	— 400
6000	6000	0
8000	7600	400
10000	9200	800

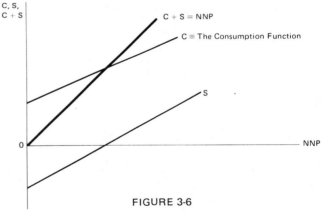

FIGURE 3-6

Milton Friedman has suggested (in A Theory of the Consumption Function, *published by the Princeton University Press in 1957) a "permanent income hypothesis" relating today's consumption not only to today's income, but also to past income and consumption patterns and to expected future income levels. This would help to explain why, when income falls (rises) sharply in one year, the decrease (increase) in consumption is generally less than we would expect from the individual's long run propensity to consume.*

We show by this illustration that consumption demand and savings are related to one another, and are both determined by the level of income.

We have shown the consumption and savings functions as straight lines although there is no reason why this must be the case. Empirical evidence gives some support to this assumption but, in any case, it makes our task much simpler without doing any violence to our theoretical analysis. Since NNP = C + S in our simple system, if we let NNP = 0, then we have 0 = C + S, and C = −S, which says simply that all consumption must come out of savings from a previous time if current income is zero.

To look more fully at the relationship between C, S, and national income, we use the concepts of *propensities* to consume and save. We define the average propensity to consume (APC) as the ratio of consumption to income. That is:

$$APC = \frac{C}{Y}$$

We are here using Y as an abbreviation for NNP, and we will continue to do so throughout this book.

The average propensity to save, or APS, is calculated as the ratio of savings to income:

$$APS = \frac{S}{Y}$$

Looking back at Table 3-2, we can now calculate the average propensities to consume and save at the various levels of national income. Table 3-3 shows the values of APC and APS. We cannot calculate these ratios for zero income, because we cannot divide by zero, but the others are quite straightforward.

TABLE 3-3

NNP(Y)	C	C/Y(APC)	S	S/Y(APS)
0	1200	—	−1200	—
2000	2800	1.4	− 800	−.4
4000	4400	1.1	− 400	−.1
6000	6000	1.0	0	0
8000	7600	0.95	400	0.05
10000	9200	0.92	800	0.08

If we add up APC and APS for any level of income, we see that their sum equals unity, 1.0. This is not just a coincidence. We can quite easily show that this will always be the case. We know that C + S = Y. If we now divide each of these figures by Y, we get

$$\frac{C}{Y} + \frac{S}{Y} = \frac{Y}{Y}, \text{ or } APC + APS = 1.0.$$

This particular measure of the way in which consumption and savings vary with income is not very useful, however, because as Table 3-3 shows, these propensities vary. They tell us only what fraction will be consumed or saved at any given level of income. If this level is changed, we have no idea what the new level of consumption or savings will be without further information. We do assume, however, that the APC will generally decline as income rises and the APS will rise with rising incomes, the situation we have illustrated in Table 3-3.

For analytical purposes, much more useful measures are the *marginal propensity to consume* and the *marginal propensity to save*. "Marginal" refers to what happens over a change in income, and shows the relationship between the *change* in income and the resulting *change* in the level of consumption or savings. The marginal propensity to consume (mpc) measures the fraction of the additional aggregate income which is consumed. It is calculated as follows:

$$mpc = \frac{\text{change in consumption}}{\text{change in income}}$$

or, using the symbol Δ (the Greek capital letter *delta*) to mean "the change in" consumption or income, we commonly write this as:

$$mpc = \frac{\Delta C}{\Delta Y}$$

Similarly, the marginal propensity to save (mps) is the fraction of the additional income which is saved. It is calculated:

$$mps = \frac{\text{change in saving}}{\text{change in income}}$$

or, expressed in symbols:

$$mps = \frac{\Delta S}{\Delta Y}$$

Table 3-4 shows the calculation of the mpc and mps from our original data on income, consumption, and savings.

TABLE 3-4

NNP(Y)	C	S	ΔNNP(ΔY)	ΔC	ΔS	ΔC/ΔY	ΔS/ΔY
0	1200	−1200	2000	1600	400	0.8	0.2
2000	2800	− 800	2000	1600	400	0.8	0.2
4000	4400	− 400	2000	1600	400	0.8	0.2
6000	6000	0	2000	1600	400	0.8	0.2
8000	7600	400	2000	1600	400	0.8	0.2
10000	9200	800	2000	1600	400	0.8	0.2

There are several things we should note from this table. In the first place, ΔNNP = ΔC + ΔS in every case. This will always be true simply because additional income (like current income) must either be consumed or saved. This implies that:

$$\text{mpc} + \text{mps} = 1.0*$$

To show that we are dealing with the changes which take place when income changes, we have written the figures for ΔY, ΔC, ΔS, and the propensities to consume and save in the intervals between income levels. That is, the mpc and mps refer to what happens over the interval between incomes of 2000 and 4000, or 6000 and 8000, etc.

It is not just chance that the mpc and mps values remain constant in the above table, either. This occurs because our consumption function, relating consumption to the level of income, is a straight line (see Figure 3-6). If it were not, we would observe mpc and mps changing with changing income levels. Referring back to the notion of a consumption function, we are now able to derive a more precise mathematical relationship between NNP and consumption, once more using the assumption that we have a straight-line consumption function.

We call the level of consumption at a zero level of income the level of *autonomous consumption*, represented by C_0. In our above example, $C_0 = 1200$. Because the consumption function is a straight line, it has a constant slope equal to the marginal propensity to consume. This means that for any increase in NNP, consumption will increase by an amount equal to ΔNNP $\times$ mpc. *Total* consumption, C, will thus be equal to C_0 plus the additional consumption as NNP goes from zero to whatever level we are considering. In general form, we can write the consumption function:

Try not to mix up the terms autonomous and exogenous. It's all too easy to do!

$$C = C_0 + \text{mpc} \times \text{NNP}$$

Similarly, we can write the savings function as an equation:

$$S = S_0 + \text{mps} \times \text{NNP}$$

where S_0 is the level of savings at zero income, or *autonomous savings*. In our example, $S_0 = -1200$.

Let us work out an example using the information from Table 3-4. At NNP $= 0$, we have C_0 equal to $1,200 millions. At NNP $= \$2,000$ millions, $C = \$2,800$ millions.

$$\text{mpc} = \frac{C_2 - C_1}{Y_2 - Y_1} = \frac{2,800 - 1,200}{2,000 - 0} = \frac{1,600}{2,000} = 0.8$$

*Mathematically, since $Y = C + S$, then $\Delta Y = \Delta C + \Delta S$. Dividing both sides of the equality by ΔY, we get $\frac{\Delta Y}{\Delta Y} = \frac{\Delta C}{\Delta Y} + \frac{\Delta S}{\Delta Y}$. Since $\frac{\Delta C}{\Delta Y}$ is the marginal propensity to consume, and $\frac{\Delta S}{\Delta Y}$ is the marginal propensity to save, mpc + mps = 1.0.

This means that 80 per cent of any additional income is consumed. Similarly we can show that mps = 0.2. Let us now calculate consumption at NNP = $10,000 millions.

$$C = C_0 + mpc \times NNP$$

$$C = 1,200 \text{ millions} + 0.8 \times 10,000 \text{ millions.}$$

$$C = 1,200 \text{ millions} + 8,000 \text{ millions} = 9,200 \text{ millions.}$$

As you can see, we get the same value for C as in the table. Actually we can only use the marginal concepts where the changes looked at are small, except where the relationships are straight lines as is the case here.

Investment Demand

In our simplified economy, AD is the sum of consumption demand (which we have already discussed), plus investment demand. Gross investment demand is the sum of the demand for investment to replace depreciation, plus net investment demand for additional fixed capital and inventories. Since we have eliminated depreciation from both Aggregate Supply and Demand, we will deal only with net investment. As a first approximation, we assume that planned investment is a function of what businessmen expect their markets to be and the rate of interest at which they would have to borrow to finance any additional investment. Therefore, investment is not influenced by the level of income. At constant expectations and interest rate, therefore, investment demand is autonomously determined and is independent of the level of national income. This relationship between national income and the level of investment is shown as a horizontal straight line in Figure 3-7.

The assumption that investment is independent of income may not be a very realistic assumption. But alternative assumptions are also difficult to defend. The reason is that investment decisions today are in part based on what businessmen expect to happen to incomes tomorrow and on what has happened in the past. How does today's income affect businessmen's expectations? That will depend on whether incomes are going up or coming down and whether businessmen have learned from past experience. Since we cannot incorporate a "learning function" or expectations function in our static model, the assumption of constant investment may stand for the moment. More on expectations and investment can be found on page 72, ff.

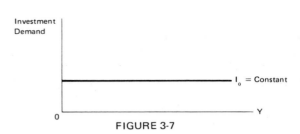

FIGURE 3-7

We must emphasize that investment demand is what businessmen *want* or *plan* to invest. As we shall see later, it may or may not be what they end up investing. Because we are not going to explain just what does determine the desired level of investment, we are dealing with a "partial", rather than a "general" model.* (We do have more to say about the investment decision in Chapter 6, however.)

Aggregate Demand Function

In our simplified economy, aggregate demand is the sum of consumption demand and investment demand. This can be shown both mathematically and diagramatically (Figure 3-8) using our previous consumption function and autonomous investment = I_0 billions.

Mathematically, $AD = I_0 + C_0 + mpc \times NNP$.

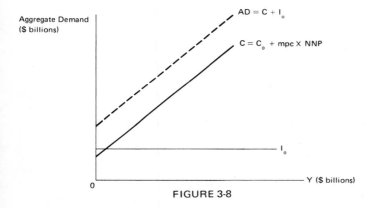

Aggregate Demand
($ billions)

$AD = C + I_0$

$C = C_0 + mpc \times NNP$

I_0

Y ($ billions)

0

FIGURE 3-8

The Determination of the Level of Income and Employment

In a micromarket, equilibrium is reached where supply equals demand. If supply and demand are not in equilibrium, price and the quantities supplied and demanded change until equilibrium is established. In aggregate economics, aggregate supply and aggregate demand must also be in equilibrium. However, the adjustment mechanism which insures that the economy moves to that equilibrium is quite different. Consider Figure 3-9 where we have integrated aggregate supply and aggregate demand. They are in equilibrium at NNP_e. At any level of income less than NNP_e, AD is greater than AS. At any level greater than NNP_e, AD is less than AS.

*The differences between economic models are dealt with more extensively in Chapter 9.

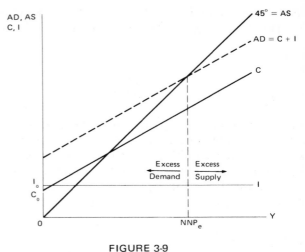

FIGURE 3-9

What this means is that at the prevailing market prices, at any income less than NNP_e, consumers and investors are demanding more goods and services than the business sector is providing. If there are unemployed resources in the economy, excess demand would call forth increased production resulting in a rise in NNP. If all resources are fully employed, the excess demand can only result in higher prices. The money value of NNP then will rise, but the real amount of goods and services cannot rise. Hence inflation will be the result. As we shall see, we cannot be sure that the system will reach equilibrium at the point where resources are fully employed. At any income level greater than NNP_e, consumers and investors are demanding less goods and services than the business sector is providing. If the economy is at or below full employment, firms will cut back on output by decreasing production and employment, thereby producing unemployment. If, however, the economy was already suffering inflation, this fall in demand would lead to more moderate price increases.

We will come back to the detailed mechanism later. Before doing so, however, we must explain why the relation between output, employment and prices is asymmetrical — why, when the equilibrium position is less than full employment, the result is unemployed workers rather than a decline in prices, while above full employment, the adjustment is entirely in the form of price changes. The reason, as Keynes pointed out, in contrast to what earlier economists generally argued, is that prices and wages are not flexible downwards. This means that even when demand does not measure up to supply at the given prices, firms do not cut prices because their costs tend to remain the same. Rather, they tend to cut *output* by laying off workers. The increase in unemployed workers does not lead to a fall in wages which from microeconomics we might suspect. Therefore, unemployment tends to remain, at least in the short run, or until increased aggregate demand is forthcoming. Above full employment, on the other hand, there is no way output can be increased. But both prices and wages *are* flexible upwards. Hence, we get demand inflation.

Let us now illustrate in detail the mechanism by which the level of income adjusts to bring AS and AD into equilibrium. Let us assume that in Figure 3-10 we begin from a position of equilibrium at full employment, A. Let us say that consumers decide to reduce their consumption in an attempt to save more. This is represented by the shift in the consumption function from C to C', lowering the aggregate demand schedule to AD'. But firms are still trying to mar-

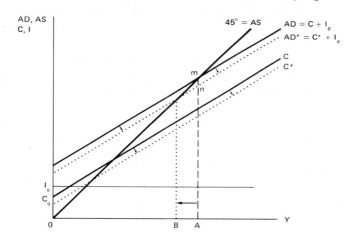

FIGURE 3-10

ket an aggregate supply to A. Thus there is an excess supply of goods and services on the market (equal to mn). As a result firms find themselves with their stocks of unsold goods, inventories rising faster than they want. In other words, firms are being forced to invest in unwanted or unintended inventories. Thus, their total investment is $I_{planned} + I_{unplanned}$ or *realized investment is greater than planned investment*. Realized investment is greater than investment demand by the amount of the unwanted rise in inventories. Since firms, in aggregate, do not normally try to get rid of excess inventory buildup by lowering price, they lay off workers and lower output attempting in

During the 1960s, inventory investment has always been positive although varying a great deal, from 111 million dollars in 1961 to 1,229 millions in 1966. In one year, from 1969 to 1970, inventory investment fell 87 per cent, although this reflected in large part a drop in inventories of grain stored in Canada.

27

this way to reduce investment to planned levels. However, as soon as they lay off workers, they reduce labour income. (They may also lower their use of other factors thereby reducing other factor income also.) This means that workers have less income to spend, and, since consumption is a function of income, it tends to reduce consumption as indicated by our consumption function. This process will continue until a new equilibrium position is reached at B.

We may now consider the opposite position with a rise in aggregate demand. Assume that firms, believing that consumers are set to buy a large number of colour TV sets, decide to increase their TV production investment program. Thus we have an autonomous rise in investment to I_0' and of aggregate demand to AD'. Now consumers and investors are demanding more than is being currently produced. Demand is now at the level B' but supply is only A'. The only way to meet this demand is for firms to sell goods from their inventories which they had not intended to sell. The result is that total investment, $I_{planned} + I_{unplanned}$ (inventory disinvestment), is less than intended, or *realized investment is less than planned investment*. Realized investment is less than investment demand by the amount of the unwanted fall in inventories. Hence, in order to reach planned levels of investment, firms take on additional workers, bring unused equipment into operation or in some other way attempt to increase output. In doing so, of course, additional income is generated, consumption rises along the consumption function, until our new equilibrium at B is established.

In the recessionary period after the Korean War, President Eisenhower publicly suggested that the population of the United States get out and BUY, that is, to increase consumption (thereby saving less) and adding to aggregate demand. So much for the Protestant thrift ethic.

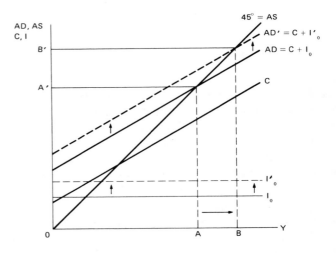

FIGURE 3-11

If, perchance, the economy is already at full employment at A, there is no possibility of increasing real output. Firms can only prevent an unwanted drop in inventories by raising prices. In this case we would have inflation. We might also suspect that the competition for extra labour and other resources would lead to rising money wages and other income payments. We can sum it up this way. From a national accounting point of view $C + I \equiv C + S$. That is, looking back on a period, the total expenditure on consumption, C, and investment, I, must always be equal to the incomes received by factors, who can only consume this income, C, or save it, S. Thus, in our simplified economy realized investment, often referred to as *ex post* (or after the fact) investment, must equal realized or *ex post* savings. Therefore, goods produced but not consumed must be invested either as capital goods or as inventory. This must be equal to savings which, after all, is defined as abstinence from consumption.

The crucial point is, however, that realized (*ex post*) investment may not be the same as intended investment or investment demand. (Intended investment is sometimes called *ex ante* (before the fact) investment and intended savings *ex ante* savings.) Firms may have underestimated or overestimated consumer demand and find their inventories falling or rising more than intended. The actual investment thus will not be what was intended. Thus, while $I_{realized}$ is always equal to $S_{realized}$, $I_{planned}$ is only equal to $S_{planned}$ where the aggregate demand for goods and services just equals the aggregate supply. Where AD is greater than AS, firms must meet the demand from inventories. Where AS is greater than AD, firms have extra supply which must be placed in inventories. If planned investment is not equal to planned saving, national income will adjust, changing planned savings until it is. When equilibrium is established there is no tendency for income to change as long as there is no change in the components of aggregate demand. This is why it is possible to have persistent unemployment if the AD and AS intersect at some position below full employment.

Therefore, in our simplified economy, the equilibrium condition is where $I_{planned} = S_{planned}$. This means that the intention of people to accumulate investment goods is just equal to the intention of people to abstain from consuming goods — there is no unwanted supply and no unfulfilled demand.

National Income and Employment

Before proceeding further, we should be very clear about the relationship between employment and aggregate income. We can illustrate the relationship with a few simplifying assumptions. Suppose in our economy one unit of labour, capital and land taken together produces $6,000 worth of output in one year, and there are 2 million members of the labour force with corresponding proportions of land and capital. At constant prices, therefore, the maximum possible output of the economy is $12 billion (2 million × $6,000). This then is the full employment point and the maximum possible aggregate supply. Consider then Figure 3-12 where the equilibrium of AS and AD is at less than full employment, in this example $9 billion.

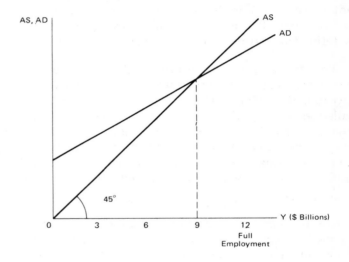

FIGURE 3-12

Two Canadian economists, Wm. C Hood and Anthony Scott, computed estimates of the total capital, labour and output in the industrial sector (excluding government and imputed residential rents) of the Canadian economy up to 1955 (Output, Labour and Capital in the Canadian Economy, Royal Commission on Canada's Economic Prospects, Ottawa, Queen's Printer, 1957). On the average in 1955, one unit of labour was combined with $8,160 worth of capital to produce $3,525 worth of output. This shows considerable growth in capital and output per worker over 1950 when an average unit of labour combined with $6,799 worth of capital to produce $3,010 worth of output (all values in constant 1949 dollars).

Using the simplifying assumption that all units of factors are equally productive, the result would be an unemployment rate of labour, land and capital of 25%. In fact, the relationship is not so direct and a twenty-five per cent deficiency in aggregate demand would probably result in considerably higher rates of labour unemployment since employers can lay off workers much more easily and cheaply than they can eliminate capital or land. Nevertheless, this example illustrates the general relationship between employment and income level.*

*A more general discussion of unemployment in the Canadian context can be found in Chapter 10.

Demand and Inflation

In our simplified example above, we have suggested that the maximum output that we can entice from our economy is $12 billion. What then happens if the equilibrium position of AD and AS is at some higher level? The only possible way of reaching the new equilibrium position is for prices and money incomes to rise so that the value of AS rises even though there are no more goods and services on the market. The problem is that equilibrium may not be reached at the expected new level. Why? The rising prices make saving less attractive. People try to buy before prices rise further. Thus, there is an upward shift in the consumption function leading to further aggregate demand and more inflation. Under certain conditions this spiral could lead to a serious malfunction of the economy. We will be discussing these problems in a later section.

We have noted several times the importance of the consideration of income as a circular flow. This means someone's consumption is some firm's revenue which, in turn, is someone's income which further becomes, at least in part, consumption which is some firm's revenue, etc. Similarly, investment expenditure becomes some firm's revenue, some person's income, etc. We can look at this in two ways, through graphical description or through mathematical derivation.

Let us take a very simple example. Consider the situation pictured in Figure 3-13. Equilibrium exists at point A. Investment initially is zero and the economy is suffering from unemployment since the full employment point is indicated at B. If businesses, expecting better times ahead,

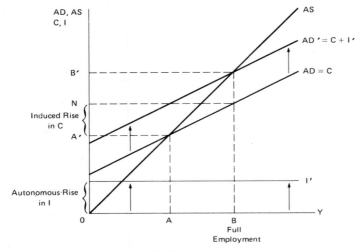

FIGURE 3-13

31

decide to expand through investment and the new investment demand rises to I', they therefore borrow money from the banks or some other agency and immediately spend it on goods. Hence we would expect incomes to be increased by the amount of the new investment demand. But the process does not stop there. Those who produce and sell the investment goods now have additional incomes. They, do not spend it all. Part is drained into savings, but part finds its way back into aggregate demand as an increase in consumption. This cycle is repeated over and over again, each time a portion equal to the marginal propensity to save times the increase in income being drained off. Eventually, the increased consumption that is cycled becomes insignificant. This increase in consumption that is induced by the effect of the new investment on income is represented in our diagram by A'N — the rise in consumption as income rises. The fact that equilibrium income rises by a multiple of the increase in autonomous expenditure (in our case investment) is the essential principle of the national income multiplier. The total increase in NNP is the sum of the increase in investment demand plus the induced increase in consumption.

We'll meet up with this same sort of multiplication effect in Chapter 5, when we discuss the role of the chartered banks in the credit expansion process.

The national income multiplier, then, is the multiple by which aggregate income is raised (or lowered) due to an autonomous increase (or decrease) in the level of investment. Figures 3-14(a) and (b) show the national income multiplier graphically.

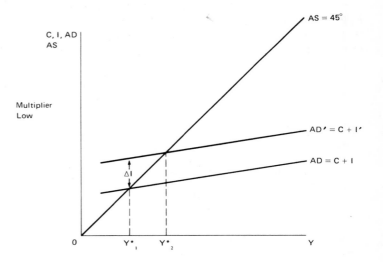

FIGURE 3-14(a)

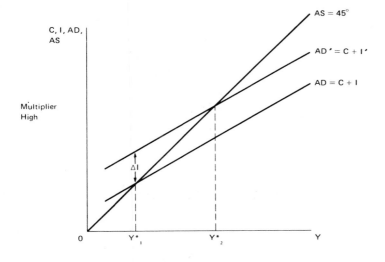

FIGURE 3-14(b)

A Numerical Example

Let us now illustrate the same principle with figures. Assume that the autonomous increase in investment is $5 million, and that the mpc is 0.8 (therefore, mps is 0.2).

Stage one — an additional $5 million is injected into the economy raising producers' incomes by $5 million.

Stage two — people receiving this new income will spend 0.8 times $5 million, or $4 million, in new consumption expenditure. This increases producers' incomes by a like amount.

Stage three — producers receiving this additional $4 million in income will increase their consumption by 0.8 times $4 million, or $3.2 million. Once more this increases producers' incomes, this time by $3.2 million.

Stage four — this further increase in the incomes of producers will lead to induced consumption of 0.8 times the $3.2 million, or $2.6 million, etc.

Thus, the process will continue until the final increase in consumption demand generated is so small that it does not affect AD at all. Figure 3-15 shows the expansion process geometrically.

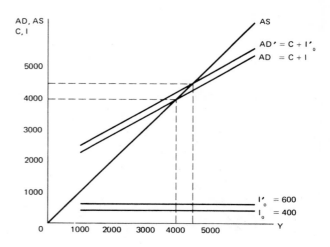

FIGURE 3-15

Mathematically, we can show what the total effect would be: stage one — an increase in investment expenditure (and therefore in income) equal to ΔI; stage two — an increase in consumption expenditure (and therefore in income) equal to $\text{mpc}\Delta I$; stage three — an increase equal to $\text{mpc} \times (\text{mpc}\Delta I)$ or $\text{mpc}^2\Delta I$; stage four — an increase equal to $\text{mpc}^3\Delta I$, etc. Therefore, the total change in income will be

$$\Delta NNP = \Delta I + \text{mpc}\Delta I + \text{mpc}^2\Delta I + \text{mpc}^3\Delta I + \text{mpc}^4\Delta I + \ldots + \text{mpc}^n\Delta I$$

This expansion (so the mathematicians tell us) can be written as

$$\Delta NNP = \Delta I \times \left(\frac{1}{1 - \text{mpc}}\right)$$

or, since $1 - \text{mpc} = \text{mps}$ in our simple economy

$$\Delta NNP = \Delta I \times \left(\frac{1}{\text{mps}}\right).$$

The term $\frac{1}{1 - \text{mpc}}$ or $\frac{1}{\text{mps}}$ is defined as the multiplier, which is usually denoted by k. The multiplier k tells how many times the initial change in expenditure demand (in our example, in investment, although the result would be the same with a similar increase in autonomous consumption) is recycled as new income raising national income to the point where AS and AD are again in equilibrium. In its general form, therefore,

34

$$\Delta NNP = \Delta Expenditure \times (\frac{1}{mps})$$

(where ΔExpenditure means an autonomous change in any component of aggregate demand).

The Keynesian Revolution

The basic Keynesian model which we have just introduced was, in the 1930s, an important break from the earlier schools of economists. It is both interesting and useful to compare the two schools. The classical economists generally did not believe in the possibility of unemployment equilibrium due to overproduction or underconsumption because of what was known as Say's Law — briefly stated, that supply creates its own demand. This "law" is easy to illustrate in a primitive economy. A farmer producing 200 bushels of wheat (supply) decides to put away 20 bushels for savings. He simultaneously saves (abstains from consumption) and invests (builds up his wheat inventories). His total expenditure in such a case will always equal his total supply. Stated more generally, an increase in supply increases incomes which must be either consumed or invested, since investment includes inventory buildup, always exhausting total product. It was considered possible for there to be temporary surpluses or shortages of particular goods but these would result in price changes in both product and factor markets (prices were assumed perfectly flexible both upward and downward), until equilibrium was quickly reestablished.

Keynes, however, pointed out that the decision to save and the decision to invest were not simultaneous decisions in more complex economies but, in fact, were different decisions taken by different people. Just because people decide to save more doesn't mean that investors decide to invest more. Therefore, the amount of goods that people abstain from consuming may be more or less than investors demand. As Keynes also pointed out, since prices are inflexible downward, prices will not decline enough to rid the market of any surplus goods but will rather lead to reduced production and unemployment. This leads to the so-called paradox of thrift: no matter how much people want to and try to save, in the aggregate, they end up saving the same amount as long as investment intentions do not change. The reason that the level of savings will not vary is that in equilibrium, S must equal I, which is fixed at the level I_0. This is demonstrated graphically in Figure 3-16 for our simple economy. This graph shows

John Maynard Keynes. b. 1883, d. 1946. Educated at Eton and Cambridge. Civil Servant in the India Office. Editor of the Economic Journal. *President of the Econometric Society. Treasury Officer. Member of the Royal Commission on Indian Currency and Finance. Secretary of the Royal Economic Society. Most famous works:* Indian Currency and Finance *(1913);* Economic Consequences of the Peace *(1919);* Treatise on Money *(1930);* The General Theory of Employment, Interest and Money *(1936). Foremost architect of the post-World War II international monetary system.*

While Keynes is most famous for his contributions to economic theory, he was a man of many accomplishments. He was highly successful, for example, in playing the stock market and in speculating in the futures markets for commodities. There is, however, one story (probably apocryphal) told about Keynes speculations while he was a member of the faculty at King's college, Cambridge. Keynes supposedly approached the college chaplain one day

how investment and savings vary with changes in national income. Investment demand, I_0, is autonomous and does not vary with changes in Y. Savings, however, are a function of Y as demonstrated earlier. Since equilibrium can only exist where planned investment equals planned savings, an increased desire to save, shown as a shift of the savings function upward, merely results in a decline in the equilibrium level of national income from $equil_1$ to $equil_2$.*

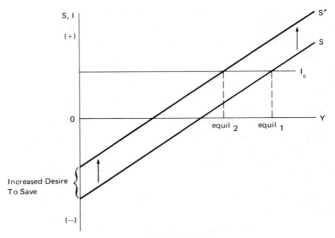

FIGURE 3-16

The classical economists were willing to admit the possibility of such a situation in the short run. But, they argued, the resulting unemployment (leading to falling wages) and oversupply of goods (leading to falling prices) would result in a rise in employment, consumption and investment. Keynes was even willing to admit that in the long run, the classical economists might be right — but as he said, "we are all dead in the long run". The problem is, how do we manage to prevent unemployment and inflation in the short run. This introduced the role of government, which will be our concern in the next chapters.

A Simple Income – Determination Problem

Given our theoretical framework, how then would we determine the equilibrium national income in an economy with the consumption function and investment demand given here.

*If we make the more realistic assumption that investment intentions may also decline as income falls (that is, that the investment function slopes upward) an increased desire to save results in a *fall* in savings since at lower incomes intended investment is reduced. Try to draw such a situation showing the paradox of thrift where investment demand = $I_0 + mpI \times Y$.

TABLE 3-5

NNP	(ΔNNP)	C	(ΔC)	S	(ΔS)	I_0
1000		1800		−800		400
	1000		600		400	
2000		2400		−400		400
	1000		600		400	
3000		3000		0		400
	1000		600		400	
4000		3600		400		400
	1000		600		400	
5000		4200		800		400

Firstly we would want to know the mpc and the mps. These can be calculated from our basic definitions where

$$\text{mpc} = \frac{\Delta C}{\Delta NNP} = \frac{600}{1000} = 0.6.$$

Then mps $= 1 - $ mpc $= 0.4$.

Secondly, we know that equilibrium will exist where $C + I_0$ (AD) is equal to $C + S$ (AS). Therefore, I_0 must equal S. But $I_0 = 400$. Therefore, equilibrium income exists where $S = 400$. This can immediately be seen to be at an NNP of 4000 from the table above. However, we may calculate it in a different way.

$$S = 0 \text{ at NNP} = 3000.$$

$$\text{mps} = \frac{\Delta S}{\Delta NNP}.$$

To achieve equilibrium S must rise by 400. Rearranging,

$$\Delta NNP = \frac{\Delta S}{\text{mps}} = \frac{400}{.4} = 1000.$$

Therefore, equilibrium

$$NNP = 3000 + 1000 = 4000.$$

If we assume investment demand rises to 600 what would be the new equilibrium? From our multiplier analysis we know that

$$\Delta NNP = \Delta I \left(\frac{1}{\text{mps}}\right)$$

$$\Delta NNP = 200 \left(\frac{1}{.4}\right) = 500$$

Therefore, the new equilibrium income is 4000 (the initial level) plus the multiplier increment equal to 500 or a total of 4500.

A Graphical Solution to the Problem

Another way in which we might answer questions about the equilibrium national income is by showing the various relationships on a graph drawn to scale. Figure 3-17 shows this method of solution. On it, we plot the consumption function, the AD schedule (which adds investment to the consumption function), and the aggregate supply function (the 45° line), to see where AD = AS.

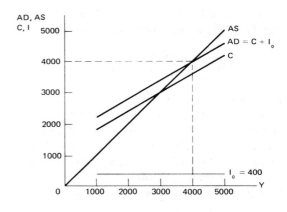

FIGURE 3-17

Reading the level of income at which AD = AS from Figure 3-17, we can see that it is 4000, the same as we obtained from the table and from our algebraic solution.

If we wish to see what the new equilibrium will be when I rises to 600, we simply redraw the AD schedule and see where it intersects the AS schedule. This takes place in an income level of 4500 (Figure 3-18) as before.

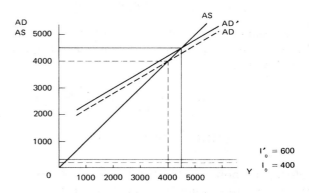

FIGURE 3-18

Summary

1.   The level of economic activity in Canada depends first on the supply and productivity of factors, and second on the fullness with which the existing factors are used. The first is the concern of growth economics. Our analysis will deal with the second; that is, economic fluctuations and policies to stabilize output at full employment without price inflation.

2.   Aggregate supply is the schedule of the total value of goods and services supplied at various levels of national income. At full employment an increase in aggregate supply can only come from a rising price level. In a simple economy (no government or foreign trade) $AS = C + S$.

3.   Aggregate demand is the schedule which shows the total value of goods and services demanded at various levels of national income. In a simple economy $AD = C + I_{intended}$.

4.   The average propensity to consume is defined as $\dfrac{\text{Consumption}}{\text{National Income}}$; the average propensity to save as $\dfrac{\text{Savings}}{\text{National Income}}$. The marginal propensity to consume measures the proportion of any change in income that is consumed and is written as $\dfrac{\text{change in C}}{\text{change in Y}}$ or $\dfrac{\Delta C}{\Delta Y}$. Similarly, the marginal propensity to save is defined as $\dfrac{\text{change in S}}{\text{change in Y}}$ or $\dfrac{\Delta S}{\Delta Y}$. The $mpc + mps = 1$.

5.   The consumption function expresses the relationship between consumption demand and national income. It is written as $C = C_0 + mpcY$ where C_0 is autonomous (consumption where $NNP = 0$.

6.   The equilibrium level of national income will occur where $AD = AS$, that is where $S_{planned} = I_{planned}$. If equilibrium is not achieved at a given level of income, inventories will rise (fall) creating unplanned investment (disinvestment). Firms will react by decreasing (increasing) output, thereby decreasing (increasing) national income until equilibrium is achieved. *Ex post* (after the fact) investment must always equal *ex post* saving, but only at equilibrium does *ex ante* (before the fact or planned) investment equal *ex ante* saving.

7.   The national income multiplier, k, is the multiple by which aggregate income is raised (lowered) due to an autonomous increase (decrease) in expenditure. It is written as

$$k = \frac{1}{mps} \quad \text{or} \quad \frac{1}{1 - mpc}.$$

Questions for Discussion

1.   List as many possible different ways as you can in which people save. Do the same for dissaving. What effect would a change in income have on the ways you have listed?

2.   Given the following national income figures, fill in the missing information.

(a)

NNP	C	S	I_0		
$	$	$	$		
10,000	10,200	____	400	mps	_____
11,000	11,000	____	400	mpc	_____
12,000	11,800	____	400	multiplier (k)	_____
13,000	12,600	____	400	equilibrium NNP	_____
14,000	13,400	____	400		
15,000	14,200	____	400		

(b)   Assume that intended investment rises to $500. What is the new equilibrium income?

3.   In country A, the mpc is .75. In country B, it is .60. Which country will have the widest swings in national income with a similar change in autonomous investment? Why?

4.   A prominent politician once went on television when his country was suffering unemployment and said "buy, buy, buy". Assuming the population did what it was bid, what would have been the effect? Why? Show graphically what would happen.

5.   During the Second World War, the government sold victory bonds, introduced compulsory savings and instituted rationing. Show how each of these would effect the economy.

6.   If autonomous consumption is $100,000, the mps is 10% and autonomous investment (I_0) is $20,000, what is the equilibrium level of NNP?

APPENDIX: Table 3-1

Gross National Product and Unemployment: Selected years, 1926–1970

Year	GNP at Constant Prices (1949 = 100) (millions of dollars)	Unemployment as Percentage of the Labour Force %
1926	7,576	3.0
1929	9,061	2.9
1932	6,798	17.6
1935	7,678	14.2
1938	8,871	11.4
1941	12,486	4.4
1944	15,927	1.4
1947	15,446	1.9
1950	17,471	2.7
1953	20,794	2.1
1956	23,811	2.9
1959	25,242	5.4
1962	28,423	6.0
1965	34,118	3.9
1966	36,500	3.6
1967	37,770	4.1
1968	39,636	4.8
1969	41,646	4.7
1970	43,004	5.9

Source: DBS. *Canadian Statistical Review*, Urquhart and Buckley, eds. *Historical Statistics of Canada.*

4

The Public Sector and Fiscal Policy

In the last chapter we developed our theoretical model with the assumption that there was no government, just the private sector. This is a very unrealistic assumption in our modern Canadian economy. In 1968, for example, the government sector represented almost 36 per cent of the annual gross national product. Government transfer payments alone provided 13.9% of total personal income. Government expenditures on goods and services represented almost a fifth of total expenditure in the economy. The control of government expenditure, taxation and transfer payments, which we call *fiscal policy*, is also only one of the ways the government has of influencing the circular flow. It can also control the supply of money and interest rates, which we call *monetary policy*. This we will deal with in the next chapter. We will now be concerned with the effect of the public sector and fiscal policy. We will continue, however, to assume that there is no international sector.

Aggregate Supply and Taxes

In the last chapter we argued that when there are no taxes, net national product (GNP minus Dep) can be disposed of in only two ways — either drained off into savings or injected back into the expenditure flow through consumption. Once we introduce taxes, however, we introduce a third avenue to dispose of national product. As we showed in the chapter on the national accounts, all of the lower income flow is either drained off as taxes (equal to the sum of indirect taxes, corporation taxes, and personal taxes, minus transfer payments) and savings, or is spent as consumption. Our aggregate supply function remains the equivalent of the NNP, therefore, except that now it is the sum of C + S + T:

$$AS \equiv NNP \equiv C + S + T$$

Taxes, like saving, are a drain from the income flow. They are not necessarily injected back into the expenditure side. Transfer payments may be considered as *negative* taxes. These transfer payments are payments (family allowance, old age pensions, welfare, unemployment insurance, workmen's compensation benefits, etc.) from the government to persons not in exchange for any factor or service but as virtually a "gift". They *add* to the income flow that is then divided between saving and consumption. The difference between total taxes and transfer payments, therefore, is the net drain from NNP to the government.

Aggregate Demand and Government Expenditure

Government expenditure demand, the purchase of goods and services by the public sector, can be treated in exactly the same way as other forms of expenditure demand and is added directly to consumption and investment demand to find total aggregate demand (AD = C + I + G). Government expenditures are normally determined by government policy and are independent of the level of NNP. The three components of AD are shown in Figure 4-1.*

The government's role in the Canadian economy has increased considerably in the post war period. For instance, between 1950 and 1967, government expenditure (all levels) as a percentage of GNP rose from 23.1% to 31.4%. The main reason for this has been the expansion of health and education expenditures. The widely held view that there has been an explosion of government expenditure and employment in the general field of public administration, however, is not valid. For a review of the development of the public sector in Canada see the Sixth Annual Review, Economic Council of Canada, September, 1969.

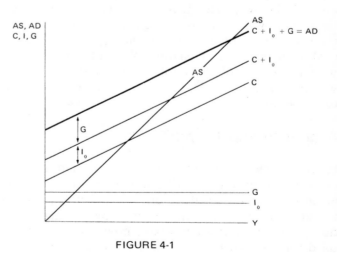

FIGURE 4-1

*Mathematically, we can now write the aggregate demand function

$$AD = C + I + G$$
or
$$AD = (C_0 + mpc \times NNP) + I_0 + G$$

42

There is no necessary reason for government expenditures to be equal to total taxes. (For the Canadian figures, see Appendix Table 4-1.) If $G > T$, then the government will have a budget deficit, which means it must borrow to finance its expenditures. If $G < T$, then the government will have a budget surplus, which means it can lend its excess revenues over expenditure. If $G = T$, the government has a balanced budget.

Savings were considered a drain from the income flow which had to be offset by the injection of investment if income was not to fall. Taxation also drains from the income flow and must be offset by the injection of investment demand or government demand if income is not to fall.

Let us consider the so-called "bath-tub" analogy. Assume that there are 25 gallons of water in the tub representing the total of NNP. If we open the drain (representing savings), the level will go down unless we also open the tap (investment) and pump in an equal amount. Let us assume we have a second drain which we open (taxes). Again the water level will decline unless we either open a second tap (government expenditure) or increase the flow from the investment tap, or both. Which ever way you look at it, if the sum of G and I is greater than the sum of S and T, the water level (NNP) will rise, and vice versa. We can now proceed to our expanded model of income determination.

The Determination of National Output including Government

As before, the equilibrium level of national output occurs where AD equals AS; that is, where

$C + I_0 + G = C + S + T$ (where I_0 is intended investment)

Simplifying,

$$I_0 + G = S + T$$

Note that only when there is a balanced budget (i.e., where $G = T$) is equilibrium now where $I_0 = S$. In Figure 4-2 we show two ways of graphically illustrating the determination of equilibrium income — where $AS = AD$ and where $I_0 + G$ equals $S + T$. In this illustration, the government is running a budget deficit so that $T < G$. We can see this in the lower diagram. Therefore, at equilibrium, I_0 must be less than S. Only at this point are the total in-

Economists have a number of ways of looking at government's role in the economy, and at the corresponding surplus or deficit. The most obvious approach is simply to record actual revenues and expenditures in a given year, fitting the figures into the national income accounts framework we set up in Chapter 2. Alternatively, we might find it more useful to look at the "full employment budget", which looks at what the levels of government income and expenditures would have been in a given period had the economy been at full employment. The government budget which receives the most publicity, the one presented in Parliament, is not particularly useful to economists because it omits such items as unemployment insurance and Canada Pension Plan receipts and payments. The important thing to remember, is that however we record government receipts and spending, only rarely will it be desirable for there to be a balanced budget.

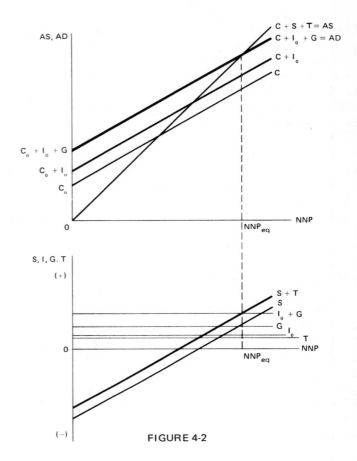

FIGURE 4-2

tended injections into the expenditure stream equal to the total intended drains from the income stream.* It should be noted once again that the equilibrium level need not be the full employment level.

The Theory of Fiscal Policy

Above we have defined fiscal policy as government policy towards its expenditures, taxes and transfer payments. Most economists before Keynes had argued that the role of the government should be limited to those public works that could not be carried out successfully by private business: defence, and administration of justice and similar

---

*This can be looked at in a slightly different way to illustrate our point. If we define $(T - G)$ as government savings (that means that if taxes are greater than expenditures, the government is in effect, saving, or that if $G > T$ the government is, in effect, dissaving), then intended investment must equal private savings plus government savings, or

$$I_0 = S + (T - G)$$

44

necessary public services. Therefore, except possibly under the emergency conditions of war, government should only tax enough to cover its expenditure. That government budgets should always be balanced was virtually an article of faith. It was, once again, the depression that shook belief in this principle. The justification for rejecting it came with Keynes' analysis. Basically, the argument follows from our discussion of why an economy could suffer an unemployment equilibrium or a demand inflation (either a deficiency or surplus of aggregate demand). Keynes argued that the government need not be bound by the same constraints as the prudent private individual who tries to balance income and expenditure, but rather should use its power to tax and spend and give "gifts" to keep the economy as close as possible to full employment without inflation. In other words, if there is unemployment, government should operate in such a way as to increase aggregate demand; or if there is inflation, government should operate so as to reduce aggregate demand.

Let us begin with the example pictured in Figure 4-3 where the equilibrium NNP is at less than full employment at NNP_{fe}.

If the federal government runs a deficit, it typically finances the excess of spending over taxes by borrowing, either from the Bank of Canada, or from the general public. To do this, it sells government bonds, and the amount it borrows becomes a part of the national debt.

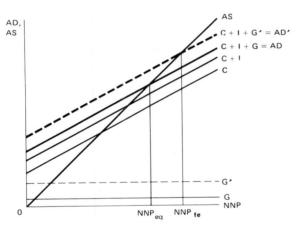

FIGURE 4-3

In order to reach full employment, the government could increase its expenditure as shown by the G' line raising aggregate demand to AD'. This would bring a multiple expansion of income through the same mechanism as discussed in the last chapter. Providing the right increase in G is extended and there is no change in any of the other supply or demand functions, full employment would be achieved. Alternatively, the government could decrease taxes and/or increase transfer payments. Why would this

During the early years of the depression of the 1930s, the decline of incomes and hence in tax revenues created severe budget deficits for Canadian governments. In this "pre-Keynesian" world, the result was an attempt to increase taxation and decrease government expenditure. Nowhere was this attitude more obvious than in British Columbia where a special commission proposed a violent cutback in provincial expenditures and increased taxes. Had government heeded the advice of such reports and even of the main body of economists at the time, the result would have been even more depressing.

have an effect on AD? Because by decreasing taxes or increasing transfer payments, the government is giving people more disposable income by the amount of the decrease in T. Given more disposable income, people will increase their consumption. This initial increase in consumption, however, will not be equal to the total tax cut but rather to the mpc $\times \Delta T$, since people will tend to save part of their additional disposable income. Thus, if the government cut taxes or raised transfer payments by the right amount (which would have to be greater than the government expenditure necessary to reach full employment), full employment could be attained through a rise in consumption.

Using exactly opposite arguments, if the equilibrium income was greater than full employment, with inflation the result, a cut in government expenditure, a rise in taxes, a cut in transfer payments or a combination of all three, could be used to reduce aggregate demand to the full employment point.

We must now devise some method for quantifying the amount of the changes in G and T that are necessary to reach the full employment point. In our initial example, the deficit in AD is measured by the difference between AS and AD at full employment — what is commonly called the *deflationary gap*. It measures the amount of extra demand that is necessary to bring the economy up to full employment. If inflation exists, the excess of AD over AS at full employment is the *inflationary gap*, the amount by which aggregate demand must be decreased to reach full employment without inflation. Figure 4-4 shows these gaps.

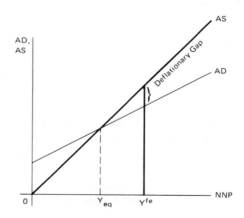

FIGURE 4-4(a)

46

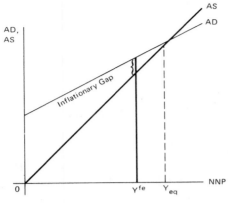

FIGURE 4-4(b)

We do know what the full employment NNP is. We also know what the equilibrium NNP is. Therefore, we know in Figure 4-4(a) that we have to increase NNP from Y_{eq} to Y^{fe}. We also know from our last chapter that a change in expenditure demand brings a multiple expansion in the equilibrium level of NNP equal to the multiplier times the change in expenditure. We are now set to calculate the necessary increase in government expenditure.

$$Y^{fe} - Y_{eq} = \Delta NNP = \Delta G \times \frac{1}{mps}$$

(where ΔG is the required increase in government expenditure).

This (ΔG) is also the measure of the deflationary gap. If we are in an inflationary situation, we can calculate the necessary reduction in government expenditure in the same manner. This (ΔG) is the measure of the inflationary gap.

It is a little more complicated to calculate the necessary changes in taxes or transfer payments. The main thing we will have to remember is that not all of the lower tax bill will go into consumption, and not all of the extra income provided by transfer payments will be consumed. This would only be the case if the mpc were 1.0, and we have been assuming that it is less than that.

The multiplier relationship is *exactly* the same as before:

$$\Delta NNP = \Delta expenditure \times \frac{1}{mps}$$

In this case, the increase in the initial expenditure is mpc $\times \Delta T$. We can thus write:

$$\Delta NNP = mpc \times \Delta T \times \frac{1}{mps}$$

47

or, since mpc $= (1 - \text{mps})$:

$$\triangle \text{NNP} = (1 - \text{mps}) \times \triangle \text{T} \times \frac{1}{\text{mps}}$$

$$= \frac{\triangle \text{T} - \triangle \text{T} \times \text{mps}}{\text{mps}}$$

$$= \triangle \text{T} \left(\frac{1}{\text{mps}} - \frac{\text{mps}}{\text{mps}} \right)$$

$$= \triangle \text{T} \, (k - 1)$$

From this we can see that the tax multiplier is not k, but k − 1. We can use it to calculate the necessary change in taxes (or, since we can show that the multiplier is exactly the same, the necessary change in transfer payments) to bring about a desired change in the level of NNP. That is:

$$\triangle \text{NNP} = \triangle \text{T} \, (k - 1)$$

This, in theory, lays out the basic guidelines governing fiscal policy to combat unemployment or inflation in our economy. Needless to say the application of fiscal policy to the real Canadian problems of economic stabilization brings in a host of problems. We will discuss these in the last chapter.

Automatic Stabilization

We have shown how a government can introduce discretionary policies designed to prevent both unemployment and inflation. In general, the government should deficit spend in periods of unemployment and run budget surpluses in periods of inflation to moderate economic fluctuations by supplementing aggregate demand during deflationary periods and decreasing aggregate demand during periods of inflation. But changes in expenditure, taxation and transfer payments are often difficult to implement quickly. Usually they involve the designing, adoption and implementation of legislation which takes considerable time. It has often been claimed that by the time the Canadian government is able to change its fiscal policy, the situation has usually changed to such an extent that the policy is destabilizing rather than stabilizing. That is, by the time the government actually gets around to running the indicated surplus or deficit, the need for such a policy will have passed and in fact the opposite policy may be called for at that time.

On the other hand, there are a number of programs in Canada and in most other western countries that tend to

Curiously enough, even if the government's taxes and expenditures are equal (that is, if the government always balances its budget), the level of government activity affects the level of AD. The mechanism through which this works is called — appropriately enough — the balanced budget multiplier. We know that when the government spends a dollar, it adds to AD by an amount equal to $1 times the multiplier, k; when the government collects a dollar of taxes, it reduces AD by an amount equal to $1 times the tax multiplier, k-1. The net effect is then $1 times k — (k-1), which is one dollar added to AD for every dollar of government expenditure.

act automatically in the way we have suggested the government should act to stabilize the economy. These are the so-called automatic stabilizers which act in response to economic conditions without any change in policy by the government. The effect of the automatic stabilizers is to decrease taxation and increase transfer payments when income decreases. On the tax side, this is done by both income and corporation taxes which tend to increase even faster than NNP, because of the slightly progressive feature of income taxes, and because corporation profits tend to rise faster in business upswings than do other forms of income.

If incomes should fall, income taxes will also fall. At the same time, if NNP declines producing unemployment, transfer payments in the form of unemployment insurance benefits and welfare payments rise rapidly. Similarly, as NNP rises and unemployment falls, these transfer payments decline automatically. In general, therefore, total taxes (corrected for transfer payments) rise automatically as NNP rises and fall as NNP falls. This means that our original assumption that taxes are independent of the level of income does not hold. If we wish to introduce this into our analysis of income determination we must therefore introduce a *marginal propensity to tax* (mpt). Figure 4-5 illustrates the equilibrium situation where

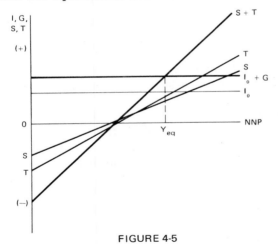

FIGURE 4-5

In 1971, Canada adopted a revised Unemployment Insurance Act with enlarged counter-cyclical measures built in. In addition to raising the general level of contributions and benefits to the unemployed, special provisions were introduced to come into effect if the national unemployment rate exceeded 4 per cent. Under such conditions, regions with unemployment rates 1 per cent or more above the average would be granted extended benefits. These provisions should increase the automatic stabilization effect of the program.

$I_0 + G = S + T$ given that T is now a function of the level of NNP with a slope equal to the mpt. We could also show that with a tax level that is a function of income ($T = T_0 + \text{mpt} \times \text{NNP}$), the multiplier is now $k = \dfrac{1}{\text{mps} + \text{mpt}}$.

As you can see, this means that the multiplier is lower than it would be if taxes remained constant. This means that changes in expenditure such as investment and consumption have a smaller effect upon aggregate income than would otherwise be the case. In other words, these automatic stabilizers tend to moderate fluctuations in the level of national income caused by autonomous changes in expenditure.

The Regulation of Aggregate Demand and the Galbraith Thesis

We have seen how fiscal policy, discretionary and automatic, can be used to prevent major depressions (or inflations). The problem is that for the government to have a significant effect, its power to tax or to spend must be large in relation to the economy. This, as Galbraith points out in his recent best seller, *The New Industrial State*, is in conflict with the traditional ideology of private business which has argued "that government governs best that governs least", a holdover from pre-Keynesian economic thought.

Galbraith, however, argues that not only has our knowledge of how the economy works increased, but also the nature of the dominant business organization, the multinational corporation, has changed to the point where it is *dependent* upon the existence of a large government sector to isolate it from fluctuations in aggregate demand that are potentially disastrous to the interests of the large corporation! (Galbraith assumes that governments are able to reduce economic fluctuations. Without the needed information and foresight, they might in fact have a destabilizing influence.)

Galbraith's argument deals with the few hundred very large corporations that dominate much of the private sector in North America. In these industries, technology has developed to the point where the decision to produce a new good has to be taken years before it is placed on the market, and involves such a large outlay of design costs, specialized capital, and skilled labour, that the corporation needs stability both in demand and in prices so that it can plan effectively for the level of output that can be profitably marketed. Thus, if aggregate demand is depressed when the goods hit the market, huge losses may be entailed. If prices and costs rise during the development stage, the final costs may be well out of line with the original planning estimates, also entailing large possible losses. Thus, Galbraith argues, the industrial system has come not only

"The regulation of aggregate demand, it will be evident, is an organic requirement of the industrial system. In its absence there would be unpredictable and almost certainly large fluctuations in demand and therewith in sales and production. Planning would be gravely impaired; capital and technology would have to be used much more cautiously and far less effectively than now. And the position of the technostructure, since it is endangered by the failure of earnings, would be far less secure. The need for regulation of aggregate demand is now fully accepted. However, its integral relationship to modern economic development has never been fully appreciated. There is an impression, growing partly out of a continuing failure to look at the process of regulation as a whole, that the business firms that comprise the industrial system have been hostile to it. This on closer examination turns out to have been far from the case " (J. K. Galbraith, The New Industrial State, New York, Signet, 1967, p. 233).

50

to *accept* but to actually *favour* a large government sector with sufficient tax and expenditure leverage to regulate the level of demand.

An Expanded Income - Determination Example

In our last chapter, we illustrated the income determination process with a simple numerical example. We will now make use of the same problem, adding to it a government sector. As Table 4-1 illustrates, the government in this example is not very sophisticated (perhaps they have never taken a course in introductory economics), since its tax revenues and fiscal expenditures are entirely independent of the level of income. This means that the government's marginal propensities to spend and tax are both equal to zero.

TABLE 4-1

NNP	C	S	I_0	G	T
		(millions of dollars)			
1400	1800	−800	400	800	400
2400	2400	−400	400	800	400
3400	3000	0	400	800	400
4400	3600	400	400	800	400
5400	4200	800	400	800	400
6400	4800	1200	400	800	400

From the table, we can calculate that:

$$mpc = 0.6$$

$$mps = 0.4$$

$$mpt = 0.0$$

$$k = 1/0.4 = 2.5.$$

We know that equilibrium will exist where $C + I_0 + G = C + S + T$, or where $I_0 + G = S + T$. From the table, we can see that $I_0 + G = 1200$. Therefore, we know that $S + T$ must also total 1200. Since $T = 400$, S must equal 800 at the equilibrium level of income. From the table once again, we see that this will be the case at an income level of 5400.

Assume, however, that the full employment level of income for this economy was NNP = 4400. By how much would the government have to decrease G or increase T to move the system to full employment without inflation? We know that the desired reduction in AD is 1000.

Therefore,
$$\triangle NNP = -1000$$
$$= k \times \triangle G$$
$$= 2.5 \times \triangle G$$
$$\therefore \triangle G = -400.$$

In other words, G must be reduced by 400 to move the system to equilibrium at NNP = 4400. Solving for the increase in taxes which would be required to accomplish the same result, we have:

$$NNP = -1000$$
$$= (k-1) \times \triangle t$$
$$= (2.5 - 1) \times \triangle t$$
$$\triangle t = \frac{1000}{1.5}$$
$$\therefore \triangle t = 666.67.$$

In other words, taxes would have to be raised by 666.67 to move the economy to full employment with no inflation.

Summary

1.   Taxes, like savings, are a drain on the income flow. They are defined as the sum of gross taxes minus government transfer payments (negative taxes).
2.   Government expenditure demand is an injection into the expenditure flow.
3.   There is no economic reason why net taxes must equal government expenditure. At equilibrium, total drains must equal total injections on an *ex ante* basis; that is, $I_{planned} + G = S + T$.
4.   Fiscal policy refers to government tax and expenditure policy, designed normally to promote full employment and stable prices.
5.   The effect of changes in expenditure or taxes on national income can be determined by the respective multiplier relationships; i.e.,

$$\triangle NNP = k \times \triangle G \text{ (expenditure multiplier)}$$
$$\triangle NNP = (k-1) \times \triangle T \text{ (tax multiplier)}$$

6.   Automatic stabilizers are those government programs that tend to increase (decrease) expenditures or decrease (increase) taxes in periods of declining (rising) national income, without any change in government policy.

Questions for Discussion

1.   Make a list of all the automatic stabilizers that you can think of. Which would you class as taxes? as transfer payments?

2.   "The public debt imposes a burden on future generations so that we can live beyond our means." Discuss.

3.   Governments facing an inflationary situation can attempt to reduce investment demand, government expenditure or consumption demand. Discuss the advantages and disadvantages of each of the three alternatives.

4. "During unemployment, the government has paid men to dig holes and fill them in again. What folly man is capable of!" Discuss.

5. Equilibrium NNP is $10 billion. Full employment NNP is $11 billion. The mpc is .8. The mpt (marginal propensity to tax) is .3.

    (a) What would be the necessary government expenditure to reach full employment?

    (b) What initial tax cut would be necessary to reach full employment?

6. No rational fiscal policy can ever exist in Canada because there are too many governments (federal, provincial, municipal, etc.). Discuss.

7. "The regulation of aggregate demand is an organic requirement of the industrial system . . . . But this regulation, however admirable, will work only if the magnitudes are great enough to count. Taxes must be appreciable in relation to income if they are to affect incomes and therewith demand . . . . So an adequate scale of government expenditure — a sufficient public sector — is the fulcrum for the regulation of aggregate demand. With it regulation of demand is relatively easy; without it such regulation is impossible." (Galbraith) Discuss.

APPENDIX: Table 4-1

The Government Sector: 1960-1970

Year	1 Government Expenditure	2 Taxes	3 Transfer Payments	4 Net Taxes	5* Deficit (−) or Surplus (+)
		(millions of dollars)			
1960	6,792	9,362	3,090	6,272	−670
1961	8,029	9,868	2,709	7,159	−961
1962	8,668	10,865	2,912	7,953	−850
1963	9,120	11,865	2,979	8,541	−770
1964	9,651	13,018	3,175	9,843	+19
1965	10,740	14,529	3,402	11,127	+306
1966	12,666	16,431	3,722	12,709	−209
1967	13,932	18,219	4,640	13,579	−551
1968	15,182	20,660	5,331	15,329	+4
1969	16,773	23,664	6,009	17,655	+1,091
1970	19,041	24,442	6,804	17,538	+134

*Column 5 does not equal the difference between columns 1 and 4 because of certain omissions from government revenues, expenditures and transfer payments. Reconciliation involves adding non-tax government income to column 2; transfer payments to non-residents, interest on the public debt and subsidies and capital assistance to column 3; and the net transfers of the Canada and Quebec Pension Plans which began in 1966 to column 3. Including the pension plans in column 5, the figures would read:

1966	+510
1967	+335
1968	+994
1969	+2,175
1970	+1,278

Source: DBS, *Canadian Statistical Review.*

5

Money and the Canadian Banking System

The Definition and Role of Money

We all know what money is, so why do we need to define it? The fact is that it is sometimes a rather difficult chore to pin down just what *is* money — and what is not! If all we had to worry about was the currency issued by the central bank, we certainly would have no problem at all. Banknotes are certainly money. But is all money in the form of banknotes?

To see that money can be much more than just the stock of currency, let's resort to what looks like a rather circular definition and claim that *anything is money which serves as money*. To decide what is money and what is not, then, we will have to discuss the roles which money plays. We shall see that there are several, and that the distinctions between them are not always clearcut.

(1) Money serves as a unit of account, a standard of measurement which permits us to compare the "value" of one object with that of another, both expressed in dollars. This means that we do not have to add apples and oranges, but instead can use a standard which can be applied to each and express the sum in money terms.

Canadians have used many forms of currency throughout their history: arrowheads; wampum; beaver pelts; French, English, Portuguese, Spanish, and Mexican coins; "official" playing cards (issued during the French regime); merchant credit notes (bons); coins and notes issued by banks and central bank notes have all served as money in Canada.

To serve this particular purpose, money need not even exist as anything more than an abstract concept. There would not have to be such a thing as a dollar bill for us to talk about the price of an object in terms of dollars, so long as the unit is agreed upon by all parties concerned. (The *guinea*, used in Britain before the recent adoption of a decimal currency, is a real-world example. There was no such monetary unit after 1813, but its value of 21 shillings, or one pound, one shilling, was agreed upon!)

(2) Perhaps the most important of the roles which

54

money plays is as a medium of exchange. Barter — trading one good directly for another — becomes complicated if there are more than a very few goods to be traded. Therefore, money is used as an intermediate good into which other goods can be changed (that is, goods are bartered for money), and the money thus obtained is used to purchase other goods (money is bartered for goods). Any object could serve as money in this sense, although some would be better than others — it would be best to have a non-perishable currency, one which is easily divisible, and one which can be readily identified as being genuine. The primary requirement once again, however, is that the medium of exchange be *accepted* as a means of payment by those making transactions.

(3) Money can serve as a store of value. Even if money is intended only as a medium of exchange, some individuals may choose to defer bartering the money they receive from the sale of their goods or services until some later time (i.e., they may hoard or save). This will be rational as long as they believe that what is used for money today will still be the money used as the medium of exchange in the future. As we saw in Chapter 3, the decision to defer demand for goods and services can have a very great effect on aggregate demand through the effect of the income multiplier. Without money to serve as a means of "storing up" aggregate demand in this way — for example in a pure barter economy — the problem of deficient aggregate demand can not arise. Goods and services would be produced only to be traded for other goods and services, or for personal use, and supply would in the aggregate be just equal to demand because for each individual, supply would equal demand. Money, then, is an important part of Keynesian theory for this very reason.

(4) Money can serve as a source of speculation against the future. If the prices of goods, expressed in money terms, should fall, then individuals who are holding money obtain a capital gain; if prices rise, holders of money incur a capital loss. That is, their command over goods and services increases or decreases accordingly. With this fact in mind, individuals may choose to speculate on future price changes. If future prices are expected to fall, it will be rational to build up one's holdings of money; if prices are expected to rise, individuals can be expected to shift out of money and into real goods, or into other assets which are expected to become more expensive in the future. Once again, this function of money plays an important role in the complete Keynesian theory, and we shall have more to say about it later on in Chapter 6.

For an interesting look at the development of money in an economic organization without a formal paper currency, see Richard A. Radford, "The Economic Organization of a POW Camp". Economica, November 1945 (Reprinted in Gordon F. Boreham, ed., Contemporary Economic Thinking, Holt, Rinehart and Winston (Toronto, 1971).

The Concept of Liquidity and the Supply of Money

We have seen that money can play several roles in the economy. But which one is *the* characteristic which tells us we are dealing with money and not just some other asset which has some of the same characteristics? We can answer this question by asking ourselves what the main function of money is, that function which we think that anything which is not money does not do.

If we take away all other functions that money plays except for its closely related roles as a medium of exchange and a store of value, we still have something remaining which we would identify as "money". In order to look a bit more closely at the roles of money in serving as a medium of exchange and store of value, let us look at a characteristic we call *liquidity*. This is a term referring to the ease with which an asset can be transferred from one creditor to another, and thus the ease with which an individual can translate that asset into command over goods and services. In simple terms, this means how easily the asset can be spent to buy goods or services, or can be used to pay debts or to make loans.

Because it is readily exchangeable for other real or financial assets, currency is usually considered the most liquid of all assets, at least within any one country. (But do you think that a one thousand dollar bill would be all that liquid?) Bank deposits which are available on demand to the depositor should he wish to make a withdrawal or write a cheque are also highly liquid, but less so than currency since cheques may not always be accepted as payment.

But there exists a broad range of assets which are progressively less liquid than these two. At one end we have time deposits and bonds, whose value in dollars is known, but which usually must be exchanged for currency before they can be used to purchase goods and services; at the other end we have real goods such as automobiles or television sets, which usually must be sold for currency before being used to command goods and services and whose dollar equivalent is uncertain and may vary over time.

In Canada, we have no "official" definition of which of these assets should be considered as money. Perhaps because the exact point at which we draw the line dividing money from near-money is rather arbitrary, the monetary authorities in Canada have not chosen to draw that line. The most widely used measure, however, is obtained by summing the total Canadian dollar deposits (savings de-

Canadians have several different types of bank accounts to choose from, ranging from rather non-liquid to quite liquid. At the extreme non-liquid end of the scale, are time deposits. "True savings" or "passbook savings" accounts, which are non-chequable, are somewhat more liquid, but pay a lower explicit rate of interest. Chequable savings accounts are still more liquid, and have lower interest rates, while chequing accounts are perhaps the most liquid, and typically pay low (or zero) rates of interest to depositors. (In the United States, it is against the law for banks to pay interest on chequable accounts.)

56

posits and chequing deposits) in the chartered banks plus currency and coin outside the banking system. (The growth of the Canadian money supply over the last decade is shown in Appendix Table 5-1.) The reason that we only count currency outside the banking system is that all notes held by the banks are (on the assumption that banks are fully loaded up) held only as reserves against the deposits of the public in the banks.* Another widely used definition subtracts Federal government deposits with the chartered banks from this total.**

It is interesting to look at the composition of the money supply in Canada using our first definition. In early 1971 the money supply was:

TABLE 5-1

	Millions of Dollars
Currency and coin outside the banks	3,351
Chartered Bank Deposits	28,724
Total	32,075

What is most significant, of course, is that actual circulating cash represents only a small fraction, just over ten per cent, of total money. Almost ninety per cent of our money supply consists of numbers in ledgers at the banks!

We should emphasize once more that *any* attempt to define the money supply with precision is somewhat arbitrary. The criterion we use, then, is determined by the use to which we wish to put the measure we decide upon. If the supply of money and near-money assets move parallel to one another in the short run, then it will not make much difference which measure we use. Over the longer run, it may make considerable difference.

Financial Institutions in Canada

Before we can see how money (however we choose to define it) affects our economy, we need to look at several types of financial institutions which in Canada play important roles in transmitting its effects.

The Bank of Canada is the federal government's agent

---

*Once you deposit cash in the bank, you can no longer spend the cash. You can spend your deposit by writing a cheque or you can withdraw your cash and spend it — but you can't have your cash and your deposit too!

**In the United States, the official definition of the money supply includes currency in the hands of the public plus demand deposits only, but there is a school of thought — identified as "the Chicago school" — which argues that for an accurate picture, time (or saving) deposits must also be included.

in carrying out monetary policy. When it was established in 1934, its corporate structure was not very different from any other bank. It was privately owned and largely free of direct political control. In 1938, the government bought out all of the private shareholders, and the Bank of Canada came into being in roughly the form we know it today.

The major functions of the Bank of Canada are broadly set out in the preamble to the act of Parliament which brought it into being. The Bank is supposed to:

regulate credit and currency in the best interests of the economic life of the nation, to control and protect the external value of the national monetary unit and to mitigate by its influence fluctuations in the general level of production, trade, prices and employment so far as may be possible within the scope of monetary action, and generally to promote the economic welfare of the Dominion.

In addition to its role in matters of monetary policy, which we will discuss shortly, the Bank is the only institution authorized to supply, replace, exchange, or redeem paper currency in Canada. This is really a very minor role for the present-day central bank, for "servicing the currency", as it is known, could equally well be performed by a private firm on a contract basis.

The Bank serves as adviser to and agent for the Government in the management of the public debt. That is, it announces new issues of Government securities, buys and sells the securities of Government agencies, and acts as a reserve bidder on all issues of Government securities. This means that if a new issue of bonds or bills cannot all be sold in the money market at what the Bank considers a minimum price, the Bank stands ready to buy up the unsold supply of securities.

It provides for the chartered banks a clearing-house function, balancing off the claims of each bank (cheques of its depositors) against claims (cheques) drawn on other banks. In addition, for a fee, it performs the same role for non-bank institutions, provided that those institutions have deposit accounts with one or more of the chartered banks to which payment orders may be debited.

It serves as lender of last resort for the chartered banks. This is why it is often called "the bankers' bank".* This means that if a chartered bank sees that it is going to have

---

*The Bank of Canada is also the "bankers' bank" because it accepts deposits from the chartered banks, but not from other individuals or near-banks. These deposits of the chartered banks are, of course, part of their assets, and are included with actual currency held as part of the legal reserves.

less reserves of cash in its hands than it is required to hold by law and cannot obtain the needed reserves from the money market, it can always borrow from the Bank of Canada, paying a rate of interest known as *the bank rate* in return for its borrowing. This almost never happens in Canada, however, because the chartered banks are usually able to obtain reserves from other sources, so that the bank rate has become little more than an indicator of trends in interest rates in the rest of the economy.

The bank also serves as adviser to and agent for the government in carrying out foreign-exchange transactions. Operations in support of the government's foreign-exchange policy are carried out through the Exchange Fund Account, which, as we shall see, becomes particularly important when the exchange rate is fixed.

The major role of the Bank of Canada, however, and the one which will receive more attention in the following chapter, is in advising the Government and in carrying out Government policy in monetary affairs. The Bank acts much like any other branch of the civil service in carrying out this policy, but it does have quite a bit of independence. There was even a political crisis over the issue of Government control of the Bank in 1962 when a conflict arose between the policies the Government wished to follow and the policies the Governor of the Bank of Canada, James Coyne, thought best for the economy. "The Coyne Affair", as it became known, eventually led to the resignation of the Governor, and there has been no public dispute between the Bank and the Government since then.

In summary, the Bank of Canada services the country's currency, holds the reserves of the chartered banks, acts as fiscal agent and advisor to the Government, acts as lender of last resort for the commercial banks and money market jobbers, serves as a clearing agent for the banks and other financial institutions, acts as agent for and adviser to the government in foreign exchange transactions, and plays the primary role of conducting monetary policy. The tools it has at its disposal, and the ways in which it carries out monetary policy will be discussed after we look at a number of other institutions which influence the monetary side of the economy.

The Chartered Banks, of which there are presently 10 (since confederation the number has varied between 8 and 41), are probably the financial institutions best known to the general public. They are chartered by the federal government, rather than by the provinces, as are most

In March 1967, an amendment to the Bank of Canada Act formalized the relationship between the government and the bank by requiring (1) regular consultation between the Minister of Finance and the Governor of the Bank of Canada; and (2) that in the case of a disagreement on policy, a written directive, to be published, would be provided by the Minister of Finance outlining the specific policies to be taken by the Bank.

near-banks. In Canada, the number of banks is relatively small, but each has a large number of branches. In 1968, there were about six thousand branches within Canada, and another 220 or so abroad.*

We can divide the major functions of the chartered banks into two categories: the credit-creating function, about which we have more to say in the next section; and the service-rendering function. As we shall soon see, these two are closely tied together, but it is useful to separate them out for the moment.

The services which the chartered banks provide for the public (certainly not for *free*, however!) include (1) serving as disbursing and receiving depots for currency; (2) providing paying stations for domestic and foreign remittances; (3) serving as collecting stations for cheques, drafts, notes and other obligations for their customers; (4) providing repositories for their customers' savings; and (5) serving as guardians over customers' valuables.

To understand how the chartered banks behave (where there is no likelihood of confusion, we will refer to the chartered banks simply as "banks"), it is useful to examine them in the same way one looks at other types of business enterprises; that is, as profit-maximizers.

Banks can be regarded as primarily producing a "product" for sale to the public: loans or credit. (The composition of chartered bank assets can be found in Appendix Table 5-2.) The price the public pays for this product is interest, which, expressed per unit time, becomes the *rate* of interest. And the inputs which the banks use to produce their output are administrative inputs plus capital inputs, plus the deposits of currency in their vaults. These deposits of currency are obtained from the public by offering interest payments at a rate somewhat below that charged borrowers.

In line with most other markets we might think of, we can make the assumption that the larger is the supply of deposits held by the banks, other things being equal, the lower will be the market-clearing rate of interest on loans. We can approximate this by saying that the greater the supply of money, the lower will be the price of money if everything else is held constant. This will prove to be an important point when we come to discuss the operation of monetary policy and the role of the chartered banks.

*In the United States, there are many more banks, and only a few of them have any more than one or two branches. In 1967, the total number of banks in the United States was nearly 14,000, with the number of branches (including the main branch) at nearly 31,000. Approximately 11,000 U.S. banks are unit banks, having only one office location.

Not only do we have chartered banks, but also quite a wide variety of near-banks, or *non-bank financial inter-mediaries (NBFIs)*. (Assets of selected NBFIs are shown in Appendix Table 5-3.) In recent years, the distinctions between the banks and the NBFIs have become rather blurred in many cases, as these near-banks have expanded their operations into areas once reserved for banks proper. We can still identify which are banks and which are not by whether they are federally chartered (banks) or provincially incorporated (NBFIs), but that does not help us very much in looking at their behavioural differences.

In Canada, savings and loan associations, credit unions and caisse populaires, trust companies, mortgage loan companies, life insurance companies, investment firms and pension funds each perform some of the functions of a chartered bank, and each has a role to play in the overall monetary sector of the economy. Because of the wide variety of NBFIs, and because they have only begun to compete seriously with the banks for deposits during the last ten years or so, we aren't yet quite sure how they affect the Canadian economy.

In this chapter, we do not need to worry about the distinction between banks and near-banks. It is only when economists begin to discuss rather complicated matters of monetary policy, that it makes any difference which is which. So, when we talk about "banks", we do not want to exclude near-banks which are performing the same functions. If a firm accepts deposits from customers, and those deposits are chequable, then for our purposes, that firm is a "bank".

One final monetary institution which we do need to take into account before going on is the *money market*. This is the market in which the various assets which we mentioned as "near-money" are bought and sold. It is the market for stocks, bonds, bills, mortgages and so on. It is not the same thing as the stock exchange, but the stock exchange is a part of the larger market for "paper" of all kinds (stocks, bonds, etc.). "Paper" is the term often used to refer to all "IOUs" for any type of loan. We don't need to talk much about the market, except to say something about the types of financial assets which are traded in it.

The most important of these assets for monetary theory are *bonds* and *treasury bills.* * In fact, when we look at

All Western countries have NBFIs similar in function to those in Canada although each country has its unique institutions. In Britain, for instance, a significant proportion of small savings are deposited in the building societies, non-profit associations founded to encourage thrift and home ownership. Recent investigations estimate their importance by noting that in the late 1950s, they financed around two thirds of the private house building in the country.

---

*Treasury Bills are short-term government bonds, maturing in 91 or 182 days. No interest is quoted on them, and they are sold in the money market at prices which are less than their face value by an amount which gives a rate of return equal to the market rate.

61

the complete Keynesian theory, we are going to assume away all other types of financial assets. Why are bonds and bills so important? It is not because in the real world bonds are all that important, but because they have most of the characteristics of other assets, and yet can be dealt with more simply. A bond is a promise to pay to the owner an amount stated on the face of the bond at the end of a stated period of time. There is thus no uncertainty about the number of dollars the owner will receive for the bond at the end of its term (although there could be some doubt about whether the issuer of the bond might default on the payment, as well as about the value of that bond prior to maturity).

The level of interest to be paid to the holder of a bond is also known precisely. For example, a one hundred dollar bond maturing in one year might have a promise to pay eight dollars on that one hundred dollars. This would mean that the buyer of the bond, paying one hundred dollars for it, would receive a *rate* of interest of eight per cent. But what if the current rate of interest on other bonds from other sources were greater than that eight per cent, say twelve per cent? Would that mean that the bond offered at eight per cent would not be sold? It would certainly not sell for one hundred dollars, unless it had some other advantage over the alternatives. We always assume that individuals prefer more to less, and it would not be rational for someone to choose eight dollars instead of twelve.

There is one way, however, that the issuer of the bond could try to sell it. He could lower its price! This is known as *discounting*. If he were to offer it for sale at less than one hundred dollars, then the buyer would get back one hundred dollars at the end of the year, plus the eight dollars in interest. Say the bond was offered for sale at ninety-six dollars. That would mean that by paying ninety-six dollars now, the buyer of the bond would get back one hundred and eight at the end of the year. That is the same as having bought a bond with a face value of ninety-six dollars and interest of twelve dollars. The rate of interest on that purchase is now $12 \div \$96 \times 100$ per cent, or 12.5%. Treasury bills are a special case where there is no promise to pay any interest payment. The interest payment is strictly the difference between the buying price and the face value of the bill at maturity. Table 5-2 shows some Canadian treasury bill interest rates during 1971 along with the prices a buyer would have paid to obtain that rate of interest on bills worth $100 at the end of a 91-day period.

If you check the financial pages of the daily newspapers, you'll often see a listing of current government bond prices and interest yields.

TABLE 5-2

	October 28, 1971	November 4, 1971	November 10, 1971
Average 91-Day Treasury Bill Interest Rate	3.47	3.37	3.29
Value at End of 91-Days	100.00	100.00	100.00
Selling Price	99.14	99.16	99.18

Whatever the face value of a bond may be, we can see that it can always be made to pay a rate of interest which will make it attractive to potential bond purchasers who would otherwise have chosen to buy some other security. Bonds, then, are just like other types of securities, only with some of the uncertainty removed.

Stocks, unlike bonds, do not have a stated face value, nor a fixed term. *Preferred stocks* have a fixed interest payment (expressed as a dividend per share), while *common stocks* do not have a fixed dividend. The price which a stock holder will receive if he sells his stock is uncertain, and the stock does not have any face value printed on it.

There are many other types of *"IOUs"* or debt instruments as they are formally called in addition to stocks and bonds in Canada today, but for the purposes of our theory, it is useful to simplify our thinking and to look at the market as if it contained only bonds.

Similarly, we will talk about "the" rate of interest, even though there are a very great many of them — short-term rates, long-term rates, rates charged to good risks, rates charged to poor credit risks, and so on. We will once more make use of aggregation to simplify the problems we would have if we tried to deal with them all.

We will assume, in our theoretical discussions which are to follow, that there is only one debt instrument, "bonds", and that the rate of interest on bonds is the rate of interest in the economy. The same sort of problems arise as when we aggregated to talk about "the" price level. We lose some detail and we lose the ability to examine changes in the structure of financial assets. What we gain is once again the ability to look at the system as a whole, and to observe macroeconomic effects of changes in such aggregates as the supply of bonds, or the demand for bonds.

The Credit Expansion Process and the Money Multiplier

We have looked at the definition of money and at some of the more important financial institutions which exist in the Canadian setting. Now we have to tie these two together. For the moment, we assume away all financial institutions except "banks", whose activities are limited to guarding the currency which individuals deposit in their vaults, and making loans to individuals who come to the banks to borrow money. The banks are willing to lend money in return for the payment of interest on the loan. At the same time, to attract deposits from the public (which is where they obtain the money they lend out), they offer to pay a rate of interest on deposits.*

Assume that there is only one type of account available for depositors, a deposit available on demand and on which cheques can be written. It does not really matter how many banks exist, nor how many branches each has. The analysis is the same because we are going to talk about the banking system as a whole, and not about any particular bank.

To start, let us assume that individual Jones in our system discovers $1000 of currency he didn't know he had, hidden away in his mattress. We know that if Jones spends the money, this will have an *income multiplier* effect on the economy, for the money represents potential AD which was previously not included in the income stream. In effect, if he spends it, he will be dissaving. There is no increase in the money supply at this point, for although Jones did not know he had the money, it was counted as "currency in the hands of the public."

Let us assume, however, that Jones doesn't spend the money, but decides to put the entire amount in a bank (to be certain that it is safe while he decides how to spend the windfall, perhaps). Say he deposits it in bank A. He now has a claim against the bank for the $1000, the bank holds the currency, and owes Jones $1000. The money supply still has not changed.

Bank A will not want to hold onto idle cash balances, however, because idle balances earn it no income. Rather, it will offer a loan, say to Smith, who wants to buy a new car, in exchange for payment of interest on the loan by Smith. How large will the loan be? It cannot be *greater* than the $1000 in currency the bank has, if the bank is already fully loaned up; and if the bank lends Smith the entire $1000, it might not have enough cash on hand to give to Jones if Jones decided to withdraw some of his

---

*We assumed in Chapter 3 that consumption, and therefore saving, was a function of income. This behaviour by banks does not contradict that assumption. We continue to assume that individuals abstain from consumption as a function of income levels, but that since banks pay interest on their savings, the public will deposit those savings in banks rather than stuff them into their mattresses.

money. Bank A will therefore be willing to lend out only part of the total. How much? In Canada, banks have found that on the average, they need to keep less than one-tenth of their deposit liabilities in cash to meet the demands of depositors like Jones. Later, we shall see that the ratio of cash reserves to deposits — the *cash reserve ratio* — which banks actually keep on hand in Canada, is governed by law.

The reason that this ratio is so small is quite simple. It is because the money which one individual withdraws from bank A to make a purchase usually is redeposited in a bank (not necessarily bank A again) by the person to whom it is paid. Bank A will thus lose cash reserves, but bank B, bank C, and so on will *gain* reserves, so that the banking system as a whole will have the same quantity of reserves as before.* At the same time, other individuals will be withdrawing cash from bank B, bank C, etc., some of which will find its way to bank A as new deposits. In general, therefore, both the reserves of the banking system and those of the individual banks tend to remain relatively constant.

This same transferring of reserves from one bank to another occurs when individuals write cheques on their accounts with one bank and those cheques are then presented as deposits at another bank. At the end of the day, the cheques are cancelled against one another (remember that this clearing function is performed by the Bank of Canada). That is why people do not have to obtain cash to pay bills. They can use cheques against their accounts as a means of payment and have the banking system keep track of the net change in reserves. No currency would ever have to leave the banks' vaults at all unless people wanted to hold onto currency for one reason or another.

It is this practice by the banks of keeping *fractional reserves* (cash reserves less than deposit liabilities), together with the acceptance of bank deposits as money by the public, which permits the banking system in the aggregate to expand the quantity of credit available to the economy.

Let's trace through the example of Jones and his new-found wealth a little further. For simplicity, assume that banks keep one tenth of their deposit liabilities on hand in cash as reserves, and that the public does not wish to hold cash at all. (We will relax this assumption shortly.)

Jones deposited his $1000 in the bank, which held onto $100 of it (10% × $1000) as reserves, and loaned $900

The recent expansion in the use of credit cards has reduced the public's need to carry currency. Other things being equal, this reduces the amount of cash withdrawn from banks.

---

*We should point out that if individuals decide to hold onto part of the currency, rather than redepositing it in the banking system, then the reserves of the banks are reduced by that amount which is withheld.

to Smith for an appropriate rate of interest. (We can neglect the interest payments in tracing through this example, even if Smith can't afford to!)

Let's say Smith uses his $900 loan to buy a colour television set from Parker, and that Parker deposits the $900 in his account with Bank B.

Bank B now has new cash reserves of $900 as a result of this deposit, and it has deposit liabilities which are $900 higher also. (That is, the bank owes Parker $900.) Because bank B needs only one tenth of that deposit on hand in cash, it can lend out the remaining $810 to Rogers, who wants a loan to help pay for his new car. .

When Rogers buys his new car and uses his $810 loan to help pay for it, Turner, the car salesman, takes the money and deposits it in bank C, which then has increased reserves and can make a loan equal to 90% of the $810. When that 90% of $810, (or $729) is deposited, it permits another loan of 90% of 90% of $810, (or $656) and so on through the procedure (a geometric progression), until the final total of reserves in the banks is $1000 ($100 + $90 + $81 + $72.90 + ...) and the total of all deposit liabilities is $10,000 ($1000 + $900 + $810 + $729.00 + ...).

In general, the formula which allows us to calculate the final credit expansion is:

$$\Delta MO = \frac{\Delta cr^*}{crr}.$$

That is, the total increase in the money supply is equal to the increase in cash reserves divided by the cash reserve ratio.

That is, if the cash reserve ratio is one tenth, the expansion is by a factor of ten; if the crr is one fifth, the expansion is five times the initial change in cash reserves.

To see just how the procedure works itself out, we might take a look at the balance sheets of the banks and the individuals who were involved in the various transactions. These balance sheets show the assets and liabilities of institutions of individuals. To show clearly the effect of the $1000, we assume away all other assets and liabilities and interest payments, and only look at the direct result of the discovery of the $1000 by Jones.

All of this borrowing will take place only if the interest rates charged by the banks are low enough to induce Smith, Rogers, Brown, etc., to take out loans. The lower the rates, the more borrowers they will attract; or, the more loans the banks wish to make, the lower the reates they charge will have to be.

---

*Expressed in algebraic terms, the multiplier is $1 + (1\text{-}crr) + (1\text{-}crr)^2 + (1\text{-}crr)^3 + (1\text{-}crr)^4 + \ldots + (1\text{-}crr)^n$ which is approximated by the expression $1/crr$ when n is a large number. The larger the number of interactions which take place, the closer will the sum of the series approach its limit, $1/crr$ (where cr is cash reserves and crr the cash reserve ratio).

66

The various banks will have balance sheets as follows:

Bank A

Assets	Liabilities
cash in vault: $100	Jones' deposit: $1000
I.O.U. from Smith: $900	

Bank B

Assets	Liabilities
cash in vault: $90	Parker's deposit: $900
I.O.U. from Rogers: $810	

Bank C

Assets	Liabilities
cash in vault: $81	Turner's deposit: $810
I.O.U. from X: $729	

For the banking system as a whole, including banks D, E, F, and so on, the balance sheet is as follows:

The Banking System

Assets		Liabilities	
Cash in Bank vaults:	$1000	Deposits (Deposit Liabilities):	$10,000
Value of loans outstanding (I.O.U.s by individuals to the banks):	$9000		
Total:	$10,000		$10,000

The important thing to notice about this final result for the banking system is that the total of deposits plus currency in the hands of the public is now $10,000. An increase of $1000 in currency reserves results in a tenfold increase in the supply of bank money, or in this case, the discovery of $1000 (which was already being counted as part of the money supply, even though it had been lost) and its subsequent circulation through the banking system led to an increase of $9000. The banking system has "created" money — with the help of the public. How did the public play a part? By borrowing from the banks, and by leaving money on deposit with the banks rather than holding currency themselves. If they did not come to the banks for loans, there would be no expansion.

Second, although our example used several banks, a single bank could perform the same function of expanding the supply of money if individuals Jones, Parker and Turner made deposits there, and Smith, Rogers and X borrowed money from that bank.

The Public's Desire to Hold Currency

We can easily relax the assumption that people do not wish to hold any currency by introducing the idea of the *cash drain ratio,* or cdr. This is the fraction of their assets which individuals desire to hold as currency, rather than as a deposit in one of the banks.

When Jones found his $1000 in our example above, we saw that by depositing it in the bank, he permitted the banking system to expand the total money supply by $9000. If Jones now decided to withdraw $1000 from the bank, he would cause a *contraction* of $9000 in the money supply.

Cash holdings on the part of individuals are thus "leakages" out of the flow of credit much as savings were seen to be "leakages" out of the circular flow of income in Chapter 3. The money multiplier, with cash drain included, now becomes 1/(crr + cdr).* If the cash reserve ratio is one tenth, and the cash drain ratio one tenth, then the multiplier will be 1/(.1 + .1) or 1/.2, which equals five. If the cash drain ratio is one fifth, then the money multiplier is 1/(.1 + .2) = 3.333.

We must be sure not to confuse this desire by the public to hold cash (currency) with their desire to hold *money.* Currency is only a part of the total quantity of money, and an individual who has deposits in an account with a bank is holding money even if he has no currency on hand at all. The desire to hold cash is contrasted with the desire to hold money in the alternative form of deposits with a bank. The desire to hold money is contrasted with the desire to hold not-so-liquid assets such as stocks, bonds, or real goods. The importance of this distinction will become clear shortly when we introduce *money* into the Keynesian system.

Fractional reserve banking had its origin in the medieval goldsmith, who initially merely kept other people's gold for safekeeping (for a fee, of course)! The goldsmiths found, however, that since only a small amount of this gold was withdrawn at any one time, they could make an extra profit by loaning out the rest. Despite this apparent perfidy, confidence in the goldsmiths grew sufficiently that instead of the gold itself, the receipts for the gold deposited with them began to circulate as money, — the original paper currency.

Summary

1.   Money is anything which serves as money; i.e., that functions as (a) a standard of value measurement, (b) a medium of exchange,

---

*Once again the multiplier is the sum of a series $1 + (1\text{-crr-cdr}) + (1\text{-crr-cdr})^2 + (1\text{-crr-cdr})^3 + \ldots + (1\text{-crr-cdr})^n$ which in the limit (where n is very large) becomes $1/(\text{crr} + \text{cdr})$. Using our previous example we can see the process. Jones deposits his $1000, but then decides to keep 10% as cash, withdrawing $100. The bank reserve, therefore is only $900. This means it can only loan $810 to Smith who pays Parker. But Parker keeps 10% as cash ($81) and deposits only $729. The bank can only loan out $656 to Rogers who pays Turner. Turner keeps 10% in cash ($65.60) and deposits the rest ($590.40), etc.

(c) a store of value over time, and (d) a speculative asset. The best kinds of money are non-perishable, readily divisible and easy to recognize.

2.   Money is distinguished from other assets by its liquidity; i.e., it can normally be used directly to purchase goods or services, pay debts or loan out without the necessity of first having to be converted into some other form of asset.

3.   There is no official definition of the Canadian Money Supply. The most commonly used definition includes currency and coin outside of the banks plus chequable deposits in the banks.

4.   The main financial institutions in Canada are (a) Bank of Canada, (b) the chartered banks, (c) the non-bank financial intermediaries or "near-banks", and (d) the money market. The Bank of Canada, the government central bank, services the country's currency, holds the reserves of the chartered banks, acts as a central clearing house and lender of last resort to the banks, advises the government and administers monetary policy. The money market is the market where assets (bonds, bills, stocks, debentures, etc.) are bought and sold. The price at which assets are bought and sold determines the interest rate.

5.   The chartered banks provide services for depositors and create credit or money. Since they need only hold a fraction of their deposits in cash reserves, the remainder may be loaned out. By the process of loaning, redepositing, loaning, redepositing and so on, the deposits (which are money) may be expanded to a multiple of the cash reserve. The change in deposit money $(\Delta MO) = \dfrac{\text{change in cash reserve } (\Delta cr)}{\text{cash reserve ratio (crr)}}$ or $\Delta MO = \dfrac{\Delta cr}{crr}$. If people hold some of the new money in the form of cash, the expression becomes:

$\Delta MO = \dfrac{\Delta cr}{crr + cdr}$ where cdr is the cash drain ratio or the percentage of new money held as cash outside the banking system.

Questions for Discussion

1.   "All banks should be required to keep 100% reserves so that when depositors ask for their money the banks will be able to pay them." Discuss

2.   "Banks and near-banks create money and the government does not stop them. Counterfeiters create money and the government throws them in jail for the efforts." Discuss. (Perhaps this is why we keep bank tellers behind bars?)

3.   Explain the differences between the desires of individuals to hold money and their wishes to hold cash. What are the motivating factors in each case, and how do their decisions affect the aggregate supply of money?

4.   Assuming that $500 in new money is injected into the economy, that individuals wish to hold ten per cent of their liquid assets in cash, and that banks are required by law to hold fifteen per cent of their deposits in cash reserves, calculate the expansion in the money supply which will take place. Show the first few steps in the expansionary process.

5.   We would be more precise if we said that the banks create "credit", not money. All they are able to do is lend out the money

they have available from depositors, and that isn't creating "money". Discuss.

6.   The important thing about the whole money/credit creation process is that the public wishes to deposit part of their money in the banks, and are willing to accept cheques drawn against those deposits as a means of payment. Show why this is true, and explain what would happen if only currency could be used as a means of payment.

7.   Distinguish between the money multiplier and the national income multiplier. Do you see any relationship between them?

8.   Credit cards are often used as a means of payment for goods and services. Should we include them as part of the money supply? Why or why not?

9.   Explain the difference between "money" and "income".

APPENDIX: Table 5-1

The Canadian Money Supply: 1960-1970

Year	Money Supply* (cash outside banks, demand and savings deposits) (millions of dollars)	Per Cent Change from Previous Year
1960	13,830	5.2
1961	15,035	8.7
1962	15,481	3.0
1963	16,861	8.9
1964	17,839	5.8
1965	19,968	11.9
1966	21,296	6.7
1967	24,271	14.0
1968	27,101	13.7
1969	29,155	5.6
1970	32,066	9.1

*Average of Wednesdays in December.

Source: Bank of Canada, *Statistical Summary.*

APPENDIX: Table 5-2

Assets of Chartered Banks in Canada; January 20, 1971

Type of Assets	Amount (millions of dollars)
Bank Cash	2,022
Other Liquid Assets	
Day to Day Loans	201
Treasury Bills	2,680
Other Government Securities	3,962
Call Loans to Stockbrokers and Investment Dealers	557
Total Secondary Reserves	7,400
Net Foreign Assets	−147

70

Less - Liquid Assets
Provincial Loans and Securities	616	
Municipal Loans and Securities	1,138	
Loans to Grain Dealers	690	
Canada Savings Bonds Loans	235	
Loans to Financial Companies	292	
Corporate Securities	836	
Mortgages	1,466	
General Loans	15,641	
Total Less - Liquid Assets		20,914

Total Major Assets   30,190

Source: Bank of Canada, *Statistical Summary.*

APPENDIX: Table 5-3

Assets of Selected Non-Bank Financial Intermediaries

	Assets* (millions of dollars)
Credit Unions	4,570
Closed-End Funds	741
Finance Companies	5,502
Life Insurance Companies	14,960 (end of 1970)
Mortgage Loan Companies	3,778
Mutual Funds	2,704
Quebec Savings Banks	569 (end of 1970)
Trust Companies	6,564
Trusteed Pension Plans	11,059

*Last quarter of 1970 unless otherwise indicated.

Source: Bank of Canada, *Statistical Summary.*

6

Monetary Theory

We have been talking about Keynesian theory throughout the book, but so far we have been dealing with only a partial model. To simplify the discussion, we not only dealt with aggregate variables, but we also dealt with only one part of the complete Keynesian theory. What were we holding fixed? When we discussed aggregate demand and its components, we looked at consumption, investment, government spending and taxing. Let us go back to the simplest case and pretend we are once more in a closed economy (no trade with other countries) with no government. That leaves us with AD = C + I, or, the level of aggregate demand is equal to the sum of consumption demand plus investment demand.

We discussed the relation between consumption and income, which we called the consumption function, and which we wrote in its general form C = C(Y), or consumption is a function of the level of income. But what about investment? We assumed that it was autonomous. That is, we assumed that its level was independent of the level of national income. In other words, we dealt with a partial equilibrium model. There was nothing in it to explain how the level of investment was determined, although investment was an important determinant of the level of aggregate demand. We discussed income, employment, and the price level on the assumption that "other things" — meaning investment — remained the same.

The Determinants of Investment

Microeconomic theory (and common sense) tells us that

a profit-maximizing businessman will undertake an investment project if the expected return from that investment is greater than its expected cost. (The reason we discuss the *expected* cost and the *expected* return is that these are the factors relevant to the businessman in the decision-making process. The fact that he may be wrong in his assessment of the situation and that his expectations may not come true, need not concern us. The fact that he may have made errors in the past will be important, however, in that it will affect his expectations of success at prediction in the present, and hence his investment decision.)

But before we turn to an examination of what factors influence the decisions of businessmen to invest, and of the aggregate level of investment in the economy, one point should be made clear: the distinction between the decision to buy "bonds" and the decision to invest. Investment, remember, is a contribution to aggregate demand. It involves the demand by an entrepreneur for real goods and services (machinery, buildings, etc.) which are produced by using available resources. The purchase of bonds and other financial assets, on the other hand, involves only the substitution of one form of asset for another — money for bonds, for example. If the money used to purchase the bonds is then used by the bond-seller to purchase goods and services, there will be a contribution to aggregate demand, but it is counted only at that stage, and not before.

Remembering just what it is that we are dealing with when we discuss investment, we can say a few things about the investment decision itself. We assume that investors examine the costs of and the returns to a project before deciding to invest, and that as good profit-maximizers, they carry out the project only if they expect it to be profitable. In a world where investors have a clear view of what the future will bring (perfect knowledge), this will prove no problem. If a businessman knows that demand for the product he produces will expand by ten per cent per year for the next few years, then he will be able to decide whether to build a new plant, to expand an old one, to continue with his present plant, or to go out of business, for example. All he will have to do is look at the costs of each of these alternatives, compare costs with expected returns, and choose the most favourable course of action.

For the businessman in the real world, the cost of any investment will be the rate of interest he must pay (or which he must forego receiving) to obtain funds to finance the project. The return he expects will be determined by his view of the future, the way he expects demand for his product to behave, the actions he thinks his competitors

Investment in the form of fixed-capital formation is one of the most volatile components of Gross National Expenditure, reflecting not only expectations of demand in the future and interest rates but many special factors. For example, the Canadian Centennial in 1967 was responsible for an upswing in investment for things like EXPO and community, provincial and federal cultural and recreational projects. These swings in investment are reflected in the wide variation in the growth pattern of capital investment in the 1960s, with annual changes in investment running from —3.9% in 1961 to +21.4% in 1964, then down to +0.8% in 1963 and then to +10.7% in 1969. In 1970 the increase in the capital investment rate over the previous year was a low 3.7%.

73

will take, and so on. These expectations will all play an important role in determining the pattern of investment, but there are too many of them for us to predict them all accurately. In developing the theory, we will have to leave most of them unexplained. (We will not hold them constant, but instead we will simply leave them out!) In adding investment to the Keynesian model, we are thus going to make the model a general one, but we are not going to be able to make it fully comprehensive.*

We do want to add what is generally believed to be the most important determinant of investment, the rate of interest, to the simple Keynesian model. We will generalize from microeconomics to assert that the aggregate level of investment in our model will be high when the rate of interest is low, and will be low if the rate of interest is high. In simple terms, as the price of investment goes up, investment demand will go down, and vice versa.** This will almost certainly be true *ceteris paribus*. We assume that it will also be true when other factors are allowed to vary.

Since we know that investment is a part of aggregate demand, this means that a low rate of interest generates a higher level of AD, other things being equal, than does a high rate. And if the government can control the rate of interest and thus regulate the investment level, it will have another way (in addition to spending and taxation) of regulating AD and assuring full employment. This procedure is the essence of monetary policy.

Figure 6-1 shows a hypothetical relationship between investment and the rate of interest, assuming that other things, such as expectations about the future, are held

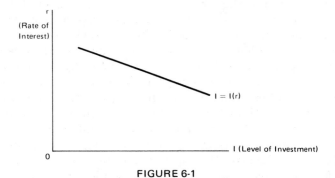

FIGURE 6-1

*See Chapter 9 for a discussion of the characteristics of economic models.
**Studies in both Canada and Britain have led many economists to conclude that not only investment but also *consumption* varies with the interest rate and the availability of credit. We will discuss the implications of this later.

constant. The *slope* of this investment function is quite important, and even more so is the *interest-rate elasticity of investment*. In simple terms, we want to know how responsive investment is to a change in interest rates. The notion of elasticity gives us a measure of that responsiveness.*

The actual elasticity of investment demand (relaxing our assumption that all else remains the same) is a matter which can only be determined by looking at the real world, but we shall assume that the schedule is neither completely inelastic (vertical) nor perfectly elastic (horizontal). This means that we will assume that lowering the rate of interest will produce additional investment demand, and that raising the rate will result in a reduction of investment.

The effects of different interest rate levels can be shown on the same type of diagram we used in Chapter 3 to illustrate the determination of the equilibrium level of national income and AD. Figure 6-2 shows the familiar C + I line, only with investment now a function of the level of the interest rate (although still not affected by income levels — this is the same as saying that investment is income-inelastic).

In 1968-9, when a restrictive monetary policy had pushed interest rates to very high levels, a number of large Canadian corporations, including a major steel producer, announced that they were delaying planned plant expansions. The reason given in many cases was that the high cost of borrowing money had made the projected expansions uneconomic; that is, at the higher interest rates the projected increase in revenues was no longer sufficient to cover the projected increase in costs.

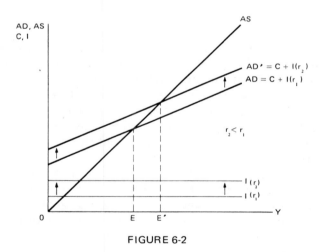

FIGURE 6-2

Figure 6-2 shows that for a given consumption schedule, the government could use the rate of interest to stimulate investment and increase the equilibrium level of national income from E to E'.

---

*The formula for elasticity is % change in investment ÷ % change in the rate of interest. That means that if we have a ten per cent change in the rate of interest (for example from 6% to 6.6%) which results in a 20% change in investment, then the elasticity of investment demand with respect to the rate of interest is 2.

The Investment Decision : A Further Note

Although in the model which follows, we are going to simplify by assuming that investment is determined only by the rate of interest, alternative explanations of the aggregate level of investment demand can be used if we find them to be better descriptions of the real world.

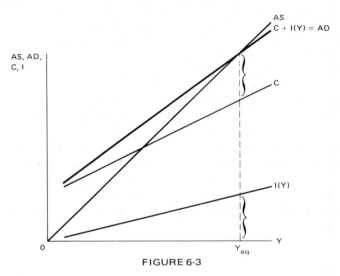

FIGURE 6-3

We really don't have a nice, neat explanation for the behaviour of investors! That's why we're stuck with saying things like ". . . it would seem reasonable", when we discuss the investment decision.

For example, it would seem reasonable to argue that investment levels are at least partly determined by the level of current income. Businessmen will be likely to invest more when they expect demand for their products to be high in the future than when they expect demand to be low. A high level of income today (or a low rate of unemployment) may lead them to believe that future prospects are good, while a low aggregate income level (or a high rate of unemployment) might discourage them from investing. Figure 6-3 shows the determination of the equilibrium level of income and aggregate demand when investment is assumed to be a function of Y. The investment function, instead of being a horizontal line, now has a positive slope to it. As we did with consumption, we can now talk about the propensity to invest out of income — the slope of the investment function becomes the marginal propensity to invest, and the national income multiplier now becomes $\dfrac{1}{1 - \text{mpc} - \text{mpI}}$.*

*As before, $Y = C + I$ at equilibrium. $C = C_0 + \text{mpc} \times Y$. $I = I_0 + \text{mpI} \times Y$. Thus $Y = C_0 + \text{mpc} \times Y + I_0 + \text{mpI} \times Y$, and solving, $Y_{eq} = \dfrac{C_0 + I_0}{1 - \text{mpc} - \text{mpI}}$.

76

If we feel that the rate of interest plays a part also in determining investment levels, we can proceed precisely as before by drawing a different investment schedule for each rate of interest, as shown in Figure 6-4. And as before, the government, by choosing the desired rate of interest,

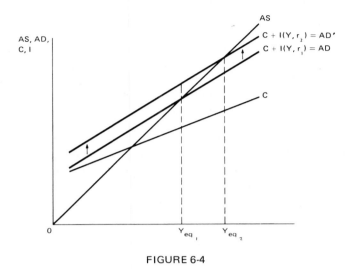

FIGURE 6-4

will be able to use monetary policy to regulate the equilibrium level of national income.

On the other hand, it might be argued that it is not the *level* of aggregate income which is important to investors, but rather the rate of *growth* of that variable. A high (low) rate of growth in the recent past may lead businessmen to expect the same in the future. This will lead to a high (low) level of investment, and in turn to a higher (lower) level of aggregate demand. (We have a case here of self-justifying expectations — by believing that growth will occur, investors take actions which produce precisely that result!)

We cannot show this process, known as the accelerator effect, on our simple aggregate supply/aggregate demand diagram because it is only useful for comparative statistics, and we are here touching upon a dynamic model of the economy. It is important to recognize this limitation on our analysis, because if the model does not do a good job of "explaining" the real world, then we may find it necessary to turn to models which deal with rates of change in order to derive valid policy recommendations. Once we introduce *time* into our models they become more realistic, but for our purposes here, that gain in accuracy is more than offset by the increased complexity.

Determining the Rate of Interest :
The Complete Keynesian System
in a Closed Economy

We claimed above that the rate of interest affected the level of investment, and that the level of investment affected the level of equilibrium national income, but to complete the explanation, we have to find out how the rate of interest is determined. In the general Keynesian theory (actually, it is general only if the economy is completely isolated from the rest of the world, so that it is not a very good representation of the Canadian case in this form, and we shall want to relax that assumption later), the rate of interest is determined by the supply and demand schedules for money. However, in turn the demand for money is affected, as we shall see, by the level of AD. That is why the theory must be a general one: these secondary effects are not small enough to be neglected without seriously affecting the accuracy of our predictions.

The Demand for Money

Although not all bank accounts pay an explicit rate of interest, and some, like the famous numbered Swiss accounts, levy service charges against the account without even providing chequeing services, they do provide an implicit return on the money deposited by providing the depositor with a combination of security and liquidity.

According to most pre-Keynesian thinking, the only reason why an individual would desire to hold money would be to carry out a transaction — to buy or sell something. Because money earned no interest, it was claimed that people would only hold it as long as was required, and they would prefer to have their assets either in real goods, which would give them enjoyment, or in some interest-earning assets, which we can think of as "bonds", although there are many similar assets in the real world. This applied to bank accounts as well as currency, although, in fact, we today include as money some accounts on which interest *is* paid.

Keynes pointed out, and made an important part of his monetary theory, that even in a simple world where the choice was between non-interest-bearing money and interest-bearing bonds, there were reasons why the rational individual might choose to keep some of his assets in the form of money. He agreed that money would be held for transactions purposes, as earlier economists had said. But he suggested that money might also be held for precautionary and speculative purposes. In simple terms, he argued that because people could not be certain of the future, because they might have unexpected bills to pay and want liquid assets available to pay them, they would have another reason for holding some assets as money.

Further, Keynes argued that money served as a speculative asset, and that people might hold it for speculative purposes. We mentioned earlier that it would be rational for someone to hold money if he expected prices to fall — that is, he would be wise to defer buying goods or services with his money until prices had fallen. Keynes pointed out that it would be rational to hold money rather than *bonds* if the price of *bonds* was expected to fall.

According to Keynesian theory, we thus have three basic motives for holding money: (1) the transactions motive, (2) the precautionary motive, and (3) the speculative motive.

The Transactions Motive

It seems reasonable to assume that on the average, the larger is an individual's income (and hence the larger his expenditure), the larger will be his need for money to serve as a medium of exchange. In the aggregate, this means that the demand for money as a medium of exchange will depend upon the level of national income. The larger is income, the greater will be the demand for money for this purpose. Figure 6-5 shows the relationship between this particular demand for money (L_t) and the money value of national income, Y, assuming that the quantity of money demanded for this purpose is a constant proportion of Y.

The clearest example of the gain to be made from holding money in preference to another asset can be illustrated by the case of a stockholder in 1929 before the great stock market crash of that year. Had the stockholder foreseen the crash (that is, if he had expected the price of stocks to fall), he would have been wise to convert his stock into money until after the price fell and then to buy back the stock at the lower price, pocketing the difference. Unfortunately for most stockholders at the time, they did not anticipate the bottom falling out of the stock market!

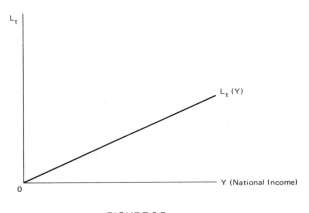

FIGURE 6-5

That is why the relationship is drawn as a straight line passing through the origin. For simplicity, we will use the straight-line relationship in the discussion to follow. Keynes argued that this motive for holding money was not related to the rate of interest.

The Precautionary Motive

According to Keynes, individuals might wish to hold money as a form of insurance against the future, which is uncertain. Because this reason for holding money is not related to the interest rate, Keynes included the demand for money for precautionary purposes with the transactions demand for money. We will do the same. Figure 6-6 shows the demand for money for these motives. We again draw the relationship of demand for money to the level of aggregate income as a straight line, but other types of relationships might be observed.

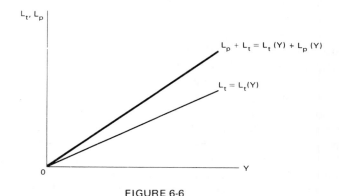

FIGURE 6-6

This diagram assumes that individuals with zero income would not hold money to carry out transactions, nor would they demand money as a precaution against future expenditures. With higher aggregate income levels, money would be demanded for these purposes and would be a constant fraction of aggregate income.

Since both the transaction demand and the precautionary demand is money demanded for expected and unanticipated purchases of goods and services, we will simplify by combining these motives together as the transactions motive.

The Speculative Motive

In a simple world where individuals have a choice between holding financial assets as money or as "bonds", money can serve as a speculative asset. Consider the choice between holding money and holding bonds. Bonds pay interest, money does not. But money is perfectly liquid, bonds are not. With stable prices for real goods, the "value" of money in terms of what it will buy is known. But we noted earlier that the price of bonds can vary, as the interest rate changes, even if they have a face value at which they can be exchanged for money at the end of their term. Consider a bond which is a *perpetuity*. That is, it has no term stated on it, and will pay the owner a stated rate of interest on its face value forever more. Say the bond originally sold for $1000 and had a 4% interest rate, or in other words, guaranteed $40 per year in interest.

If the rate of interest on equally safe alternative assets in the system is also 4%, then a buyer of bonds will be indifferent between this one and those alternatives. But say the government takes action to raise the rate of interest from 4% to 6% in order to cut down on investment in order to combat inflationary pressures. That is, alternative securities will now be issued with rates of interest at 6%, not 4%.

A bond purchaser with $1000 to spend could now obtain a newly issued $1000 bond with an annual interest payment of $60 (6% of $1000). The holder of the 4% bond is getting only $40 in interest. What would happen? The holder of the bond paying $40 would try to sell his bond in order to obtain one with a higher rate of interest. But no one would want to pay him $1000 for the bond, since that would pay them only 4% interest per year, and they could buy other bonds and obtain 6%. The result, then, would be to bid the selling price of the bond down to a level P_b which would provide a 6% rate of return on the investment. That would be the price where

$$\frac{\text{Interest}}{P_b} = 6\%, \text{ or } \frac{40}{P_b} = \frac{6}{100}, \text{ or } P_b = \$666.67.$$

This means that the person holding the bond when the rate of interest in the system rose suffered a capital loss. And if that individual had *expected* the rate of interest to rise, he would have been wise to try to sell his bond first, and hold his assets in money form until the change actually took place, when he could once more buy a bond, this time paying $60 for every $1000 he invested.

Just the opposite would occur if the rate of interest declined while our individual was holding the 4% bond with a face value of $1000. Now assume the rate of interest in the economy fell from 4% to 3%. New $1000 bonds would pay annual interest of $30. Therefore, people would prefer the 4% bond to alternative bonds at a price of $1000 because they would pay only 3%. The increased demand for this bond would bid up its price until it yielded a rate of interest equal to 3%, when bond purchasers would be indifferent between it and alternative bonds. That is,

Perpetual bonds, called consols, *were actually issued in Britain in the 19th Century. They had no real face value and in practice are irredeemable. They pay 2½% on the original selling value of £100. That is, the investor gets £2½ per year for each consol. How much is the bond worth today? This all depends on the current interest rate. If we assume the appropriate rate is now 8%, the price of the consol would be:*

$$\frac{£2.5}{.08} = £31.25, \text{ less than a}$$

third the original price.

81

when the price of this bond reached the level where

$$\frac{\text{Interest}}{P_b} = \frac{3}{100} \text{ or } \frac{40}{P_b} = \frac{3}{100}, \text{ or } P_b = \$1333.33.$$

A person holding the 4% bond when the rate of interest fell to 3% would thus obtain a capital gain of $333.33, or one third of the purchase price.

If the rate of interest is expected to fall, people will thus try to buy bonds, run down their stocks of money, and obtain the capital gains.

We now have most of the information we need to relate the demand for money for speculative purposes, which Keynes gave the name *liquidity preference* to the rate of interest. We know that when the rate of interest is expected to *rise*, people will want to hold money; when the rate of interest is expected to *fall*, people will wish to hold bonds. This refers to changes in the rate of interest, however, and we want to relate the demand for money to the *level* of the rate of interest.

In order to do this, we have to introduce the notion of a *normal rate of interest*. It is defined as the rate which people think is "normal", and toward which they expect the rate to move. Each person may have his own idea of just where that normal rate may be. But the higher the actual rate is, the fewer will be the people who expect it to rise still more; and the lower is the actual rate, the more people there will be who expect it to rise.

From this, we can infer that if the interest rate is "low", people will wish to move out of bonds and into money. If the rate is "high", people will wish to hold bonds and not money. Figure 6-7 shows the relationship between the level of the rate of interest and the demand for money (we could equally well show the demand for bonds as a function of the rate of interest).

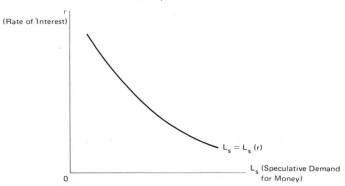

FIGURE 6-7

82

The exact shape of the liquidity preference schedule shown in Figure 6-7 is uncertain, since it depends upon *expectations*. Keynes suggested that the schedule would slope downward to the right, as shown above, but that, at some low rate of interest, the curve would become horizontal. This horizontal section would occur if at some stage every person in society was convinced that the rate of interest had gone as low as it could fall, and hence everyone believed that it would rise in the future. That would mean that everyone expected capital losses if they held bonds, and hence no one would want to hold bonds, whatever their price.

This situation Keynes called a *liquidity trap*. By this he meant to indicate that the demand for liquid assets was so high that no one would hold bonds, and hence the monetary authorities could not lower the rate of interest. Monetary policy would then be useless. We shall see how important this might be in the complete Keynesian model, but we must remember that the actual shape of the liquidity preference schedule can only be determined by looking at the real-world behaviour of individuals. Figure 6-8 illustrates the case where the liquidity preference schedule has a horizontal segment and thus gives rise to a liquidity trap.

Keynes didn't really say he thought that there was a liquidity trap built into the demand for money schedule, just that this sort of a situation could arise.

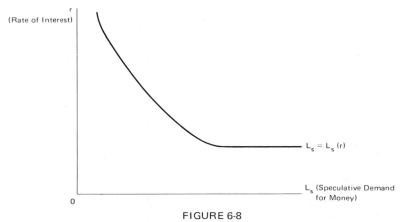

FIGURE 6-8

The Supply of Money

We mentioned earlier that the supply of money could be defined as the sum of currency in the hands of the public plus chequeable deposits at the banks or near-banks. All we need to do to complete the monetary side of the Keynesian theory is to add this supply of money to the demands for money we have been discussing. How is the money supply determined? The quantity of currency in the system is determined by the monetary authorities —

the Bank of Canada, in other words. The supply of deposits we saw was determined by the supply of currency, the demand on the part of the public to hold currency (*not* to hold *money*, it will be remembered), and the cash reserve ratio which the banks have to maintain. We assume that the banks adjust their rates of interest on loans so that they stay fully loaned up. This means that we can calculate the money supply by using the money multiplier we discussed in Chapter 5, and that the monetary authorities, by controlling the supply of currency, can control the total supply of money. We will assume that the money supply is *entirely a policy variable*, therefore, and is simply something which is set by the central bank. The supply is not related to the level of income, nor is it related to the rate of interest (unless of course the monetary authorities choose to regulate the supply in such a way). For any given monetary policy the money supply can be illustrated as in Figure 6-9.

The money supply has been a policy variable in Canada since 1933, when the gold standard was officially abandoned. As long as a country's currency must be backed by gold, its money supply can change only if the supply of gold reserves changes. This leaves much to the chance discovery of gold-bearing ore, to changes in international trading relationships, and so on, an obviously undesirable situation for a country wishing to pursue an independent economic policy.

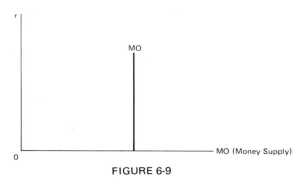

FIGURE 6-9

Equilibrium of Supply and Demand for Money

According to our theory, we have two reasons why the public will demand money: for transactions purposes, and for speculative purposes. The supply of money we have claimed to be set by the monetary authorities. What then will be the "price" of money which makes supply just equal to demand?

We have a problem here in trying to find that price (which will be the opportunity cost of holding money, or the rate of interest), because the demand for money is not only a function of the rate of interest, but *also* of the level of national income.

In a partial equilibrium framework, we could say that holding aggregate income constant (holding the transactions demand constant), equilibrium of supply and demand would give a rate of interest. Figure 6-10 shows this case.

84

The transactions demand is interest-rate inelastic (that is, it is constant no matter what the rate of interest is), while the speculative demand is a function of the rate of interest. Adding these demands together, we get an aggregate demand for money which is a function of the rate of interest, other things being equal.

The supply of money, determined by policy decisions on the part of the monetary authorities, is shown as a constant MO. The equilibrium rate of interest is determined by the intersection of the supply and demand curves at the level r* in Figure 6-10.

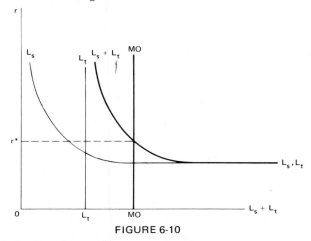

FIGURE 6-10

But L_t has been drawn under the assumption that the level of national income remains constant. Each level of national income has a particular transactions demand for money. And that means that for each level of national income, there is a different *total* demand for money, as shown in Figure 6-11.

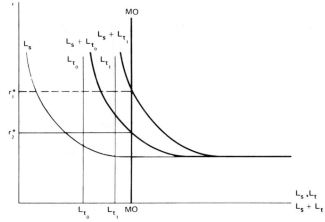

FIGURE 6-11

85

For any given money supply level, MO, this means that there could be *many* rates of interest depending on the level of national income which would make the supply of and demand for money equal. This is, of course, because the demand for money changes with each change in income. Instead of finding *a* rate of interest, therefore, we find one rate of interest for each possible level of national income. In a partial equilibrium setting, holding national income constant, we thus have *a* solution. To find the more general result, we need to look at other variables in the system which are related to the level of national income and the interest rate; that is, at savings and investment.

The Quantity Theory of Money

Keynesian theory, as we pointed out in Chapter 3, is "short run" in nature. That is, it is useful in "explaining" deviations from the desired full-employment, stable price equilibrium of the economy. However, while it is safe to say that almost all economists are to some degree or other "Keynesian", the long-run tendencies of the economy should not be ignored. Further, there is a growing belief that the long-run theory of pre-Keynesians is useful — with some modification — in looking at short-run events as well. As we shall see, a critical difference between the two views of the world which emerge from the models is in the role played by money.

The *quantity theory of money* forms the basis of the long-run theory. Looking back on any period of time, the money value of goods and services exchanged in the economy must be equal to the number of dollars times the average number of times each dollar was spent. If we let M be the number of dollars (i.e., the level of the money supply); V be the average number of times a dollar was spent (*the velocity of money*); P be the price level in the economy; and T be the total production of goods and services, then we can write the identity:

$$M \times V \equiv P \times T.$$

If we claim that V is a constant, while T is the full employment level of production, we now have a *theory* which says that the price level in the economy is determined by the level of the money supply. We now can write

$$MV = PT \quad \text{or} \quad P = \frac{MV}{T}.$$

That is, if in the long run the economy tends toward the full employment position, changing the money supply will affect only the price level. This, of course, assumes that T (the total production of goods and services) remains constant as well. But this is unrealistic in modern economies where national output tends to rise every year. If the money supply remained constant while output increased, our theory tells us that (V remaining constant), the price level would fall. But this is not in accord with real world experience and is probably undesirable from the point of view of stabilizing the economy and encouraging growth. Therefore, we could recommend from this long run theory that the money supply should be increased at the same rate as the physical output of the economy to maintain general price stability.

In contrast to this *long run* theory, we can use the same equation for quite different purposes, to "explain" *short run* fluctuations in the level of output and prices as a result of changes in the supply of money. Again, we must assume that V remains constant. If we begin in a state of less than full employment, and the price level is assumed to be fixed in the short run, then changes in M must result in changes in T. In its simplest form, therefore, raising the money supply should produce full employment. And while in the long run there may be adjustments in the market for labour and the market for goods and services (through adjustments in wages and the price level), in the short run the level of economic activity is hypothesized to respond directly to the money supply level. That is, we can write

$$T = \frac{MV}{P},$$

where T is no longer assumed to be the full employment position. If, however, the economy is already at the full employment level, increasing M could only produce rising prices (since T cannot rise).

The prime weakness of this theory as a *short run* explanation is the assumption that V is constant. There is evidence that in the real world, the velocity of money tends to change over the course of the business cycle in a fairly regular fashion and may even change in a secular fashion over time through the use of instruments that conserve on the use of money for transactions — such as credit cards.

We could of course relax the assumption that V remains a constant, and there is evidence that in the real world the velocity of money tends to change over the course of the

The German hyper-inflation of the 1920s illustrates the connection between the money supply and the price level. Each increase in the money supply (financing government deficits), led to a price increase. As buyers began to expect *price increases, they rushed to spend their money, thus pushing prices up even further by increasing the velocity as well as the quantity of money, leading to further attempts at rapid spending, further increases in prices, and so on — with a final increase in prices of 18 trillion per cent!*

business cycle in a fairly regular fashion. But there is still likely to be some relationship between prices, or the level of economic activity (or both!) and the money supply unless changes in V just offset changes in M.

What is it about the role of money which is important in the simple quantity theory? It is that the *only* reason individuals hold money is to make purchases. That is, the transactions motive plus the precautionary motive fully describe the demand for money. Individuals holding "excess" money simply have not yet made the purchases with it that they intend to. And if in the aggregate there is "excess" money, the result will be an attempt on the part of the individuals involved to run down their stocks of money by spending them, not on bonds as will be the case under Keynesian conditions, but on real goods and services. There is thus a direct link between money and aggregate demand, a link which in Keynesian theory is modified by the intercession of the rate of interest. If we remove the speculative demand for money from the Keynesian theory, as we would probably do in building a long run theory, then the two models produce rather similar results. This is not meant to imply that the only difference between Keynes' and Classical or neo-Classical theory is the speculative demand for money, but to point out that this is one important area of difference between them.

Summary

1.   The level of investment is dependent on the rate of interest, rising as the interest rate falls.
2.   The demand for money is made up of two demands — money to carry out transactions (anticipated or unanticipated) and money to speculate against a change in the interest rate. The transactions demand is a function of income, rising as income rises. The speculative demand is a function of the interest rate, high when interest rates are low and expected to rise, and low when interest rates are high and expected to fall. This behaviour is known as *liquidity preference.*
3.   The supply of money is purely a function of the monetary policy of the government or its agent, the Bank of Canada.
4.   For a general equilibrium situation in both real and monetary parts of the economy, it is necessary not only to have S = I (equilibrium in the real sector), but also have the demand for money (L) equal to the supply of money (MO), (equilibrium in the monetary sector).
5.   In the long run, if we assume that the velocity of money (V) is constant, and the economy remains at full employment (at output level T), then the price level (P) depends only on the level of the money supply (M) according to the formula $P = \dfrac{MV}{T}$.
6.   In the short run, if prices and the velocity of money remain

constant, we can predict changes in the level of output (and hence employment) according to the relationship $T = \dfrac{MV}{P}$. Under these conditions, the government could regulate employment by adjusting the supply of money.

Questions for Discussion

1. Explain the difference between investing and buying bonds.

2. "If they have any choice, people will always prefer to hold bonds rather than money, because holding money pays no rate of interest. People will only hold money long enough to make transactions with it." Discuss.

3. Explain the relationship between the rate of interest and the level of investment demand. Distinguish this from the relationship between the rate of interest and the desire to hold bonds.

4. Distinguish between liquidity preference and the preference for beer and gin.

5. Explain how the government can use monetary policy to regulate the level of AD. How do policy-makers determine how large a change in the supply of money will be needed to bring about the desired change?

6. Explain the difference in effect on the economy between a government expenditure and an increase in the supply of money by the government.

7. "In the Keynesian theory, the rate of interest is important because it influences the level of investment and thus the level of aggregate demand. In the neo-Classical (short-run quantity) theory, it is the money supply and not the interest rate which is important; the interest rate is simply the price which emerges as a result of the interaction of the supply of and demand for investment funds." Discuss.

APPENDIX: A Graphical Presentation of the Complete Keynesian System in a Closed Economy (The Hicks-Hansen Formulation)

We have now talked about all of the separate parts of the complete Keynesian system, and the time has come to fit them together. We will divide the system into two parts: the "real" sector, including the decisions of individuals to save or invest, and the "monetary" sector, concerning the supply of and demand for money.

The Real Sector

The relationships discussed in Chapter 3 between the level of national income and the level of consumption and savings in the aggregate, and our discussion of the investment function, make up the real sector. Figure 6-12 shows savings as a function of income.

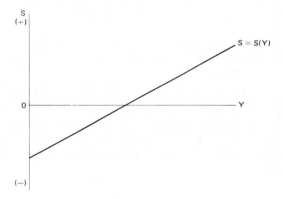

FIGURE 6-12

Figure 6-13 shows investment as a function of the rate of interest.

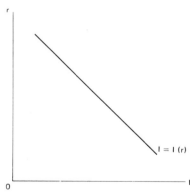

FIGURE 6-13

90

We know from our discussion in Chapter 3 that savings and investment must be equal if the economy is to be in equilibrium. If we hold the rate of interest constant and hence hold investment constant, we can derive a partial equilibrium solution, which is what we did in Chapter 3. But if the rate of interest — and thus investment — can vary, this means that for each rate of interest, there is an equilibrium level of national income.

We can fit the relationships in Figure 6-12 and 6-13 together graphically in the following way:

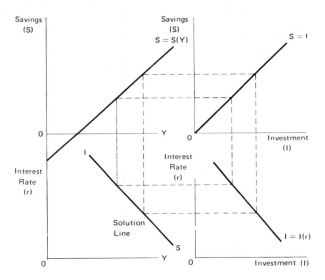

FIGURE 6-14

We make use of the equilibrium condition savings = investment in order to link the two diagrams and graphically *solve* them. What we get for a solution, however, is a *line* rather than a *point*. This is simply the same as saying that for each level of the rate of interest, there is a particular level of national income for which S = I. Or, if we wish, for each level of national income, there is a rate of interest for which S = I.* We label this curve the "IS" curve. So far, we do not have enough information to determine a particular solution to the problem, and we now wish to add the monetary sector in order to come up with that solution.

*In mathematical form, the problem is to solve three equations in four unknowns. The solution is a line (not necessarily a straight line). The unknowns are the rate of interest, the level of investment, the level of national income, and the level of savings. In equation form, we have I = I(r), S = S(Y), and S = I. The solution is S(Y) = I(r) which is one equation in two unknowns and is represented by the IS curve shown on the axes r and Y.

The Monetary Sector

Both the real and the monetary sectors use dollar values as measuring rods. In the first instance, however, we are dealing with decisions to consume and save; while in the second, we are discussing the decisions of individuals to hold money rather than bonds.

In order to discuss the monetary influence of the level of national income and the rate of interest separately, we will keep the two demands for money separated. Thus we have the demand for money for transactions purposes as a function of national income, and the demand for money for speculative purposes as a function of the rate of interest, plus an equilibrium condition which says that the sum of transactions demand plus speculative demand must just be equal to the supply of money.* Figure 6-15 shows the speculative demand; Figure 6-16 shows the transactions demand, and Figure 6-17 shows the quantity of money available for any combination of speculative and transactions purposes.

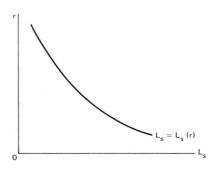

FIGURE 6-15

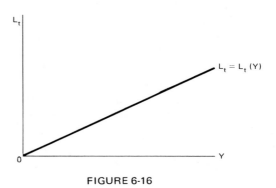

FIGURE 6-16

*This is just the same as a budget constraint, because it tells us how much money is available to be "spent" for transactions and speculative balances.

92

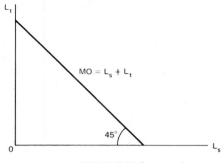

FIGURE 6-17

When we combine these three relationships* graphically, we obtain Figure 6-18 which once again gives us a line as the solution. And once again the relationship is the set of combinations of income levels and interest rates which are points of equilibrium in the monetary sector. Supply of and demand for money are equal for combinations of incomes and rates of interest specified.

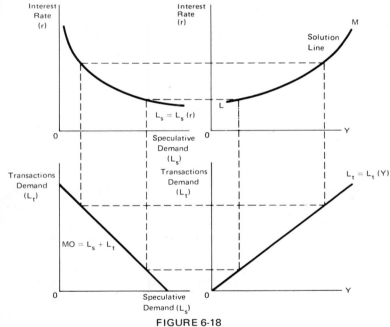

FIGURE 6-18

We call this the LM curve, to indicate that it specifies the equilibrium conditions for the demand for liquidity (money) and the supply of money.

*In equation form $L_s = L_s(r)$; $L_t = L_t(Y)$; $L_s + L_t = MO$. Once again we have three equations and four unknowns, and the solution is a line, not a point.

The Real and Monetary Sectors Combined

Both the IS and LM curves are drawn to show equilibrium conditions of income and interest rates, so that we can combine them to find the point where both markets are in equilibrium at the same time. This is the same thing as finding a *general* equilibrium position for the system. To make the procedure clear, we will draw in all of the relationships between variables and show the IS and LM curve derivations once more. Figure 6-19 illustrates the general equilibrium situation.

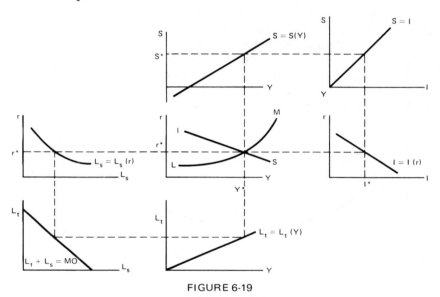

FIGURE 6-19

In each of the real and monetary sectors, we had four unknowns and three equations. If we look at the combined system, we will see that we now have six equations (three from each sector) and six unknowns.* We mentioned

*The variables are savings, investment, the rate of interest, the level of national income, the speculative demand for money, and the transactions demand for money. The equations are

$$S = S(Y)$$
$$I = I(r)$$
$$L_s = L_s(r)$$
$$L_t = L_t(Y)$$
$$S = I$$
$$L_s + L_t = MO$$

We can either solve all of these at the same time, or, as we have done above, break them down into two parts, each yielding one equation in two unknowns, and solve these two equations (the IS and LM equations) in two unknowns (r and Y) to obtain the same answer.

94

earlier that this is not a guarantee that a general equilibrium will exist, but it is a necessary condition for one.

From our central diagram, we can pick out the equilibrium rate of interest and the equilibrium level of national income. With these values in mind, we can pick out the equilibrium levels of investment, savings, and money held for transactions and speculative purposes.

We should remember once again, however, that simply because we have an equilibrium position (even a general one) we are not necessarily at full employment. We have no guarantee in the model that the equilibrium level of national income is the full employment level, so that there is still room for government intervention in the economy's workings. In fact, by bringing in the monetary side of the economy, we have simply introduced another policy tool which a government might use to regulate the level of AD.

Fiscal Policy in the General Model

In introducing government our equilibrium condition is no longer where $I = S$ but rather where $I + G = S + T$. However, to simplify we can say that $T - G$ is government saving. (If the government's income, T, is greater than its expenditure G then it is doing a form of saving. If $G > T$, then it is dissaving.) Then equilibrium will exist where $I = S +$ government saving. For our purposes $S +$ government saving will be written as S_t.

Let us say that the economy reaches an equilibirum position at a level Y^* which is less than the full employment level, and the government has committed itself to ensuring full employment. What can it do in this model to achieve that position?

We can use the 7-diagram presentation to show what effects there would be if the government followed various policies. The immediate effects of the policies are shown by shifts in the various relationships. For example, increased government spending, ΔG, not balanced by increased taxes can be shown as a shift in the savings function, (i.e., $T - G$, or government saving becomes less). Aggregate consumption (including government consumption) demand is higher at each level of income than was previously the case, so that the aggregate savings must be lower. The savings function is shifted downward to the right, as shown in Figure 6-20. None of the other relationships will change.

In the real world, different individuals and different groups have different propensities to save and consume. This means that when we consider a government tax or expenditure policy, we need to know which group pays those taxes or which group receives the government expenditure; the mpc and mps for the economy as a whole will be different for different income patterns.

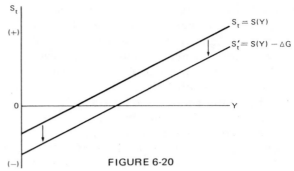

FIGURE 6-20

We can use this new savings schedule to derive a new IS curve, which will be to the right of the old IS curve as shown in Figure 6-21. The new general equilibrium position will be at the level shown where the new IS curve intersects the LM curve at Y**. Unless the LM curve happens to have a vertical portion at the original level of national income*, there will be a tendency for national income to increase. What the shape of the LM curve actually is can only be determined empirically but we will assume that it is not likely to be vertical under most conditions.

When you work with these diagrams, try to make sure you don't confuse shifts *in one of the curves with movements* along *a curve. In Figure 6-21, when the IS curve shifts, there is a movement along the LM curve. That is, the LM curve is the same, but we move to a new position on it. More money is demanded for transactions purposes after the IS curve shifts, raising the equilibrium income level, and less is demanded for speculative purposes as the interest rate rises, but the LM schedule itself is unchanged.*

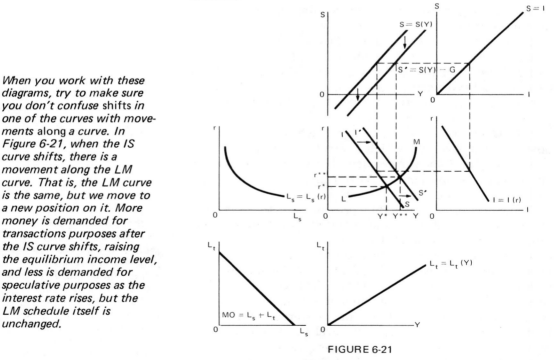

FIGURE 6-21

*Try to see from the diagrams of the monetary sector how this could come about. Hint: where does the liquidity preference schedule have a vertical segment?

96

It is important to note, however, that by increasing its spending without increasing taxation, the government reduced the supply of savings available for private investors, and thus caused a rise in the rate of interest (to r^{**}) and a lower level of investment. It also caused a change in the amounts of money held for speculative and transactions purposes, but that does not matter here. The point is that a *part* of government spending was at the expense of private investment, which fell from I^* to I^{**}. If the LM curve were vertical, *all* of it would have been at the expense of investment, and aggregate demand would not have increased at all.

Actually, this discussion has made an assumption that we should look at more closely: that none of the other variables or relationships changes. In fact, if the government spends more with no increase in revenues, then it either must be increasing the supply of money (which shifts MO to the right) or it must be selling government securities (bonds) to obtain the money to spend. The above situation occurs when the government sells bonds to finance its expenditure. The increased supply of bonds on the market tends to depress their price, and thus tends to raise the rate of interest. That is exactly what we have shown. The rise in the rate of interest discourages investment and offsets part of the government's expansionary activity. Only if the money supply is permitted to expand by enough to satisfy the additional transactions demand generated by increased income, and to leave the interest rate unchanged, will the full effect of fiscal policy be felt. This means that in Chapter 3, by ignoring this problem, we overstated the multiplier effect of government expenditures. Figure 6-22 on the following page shows a combination of monetary and fiscal policies which gives the fiscal effect of the full multiplier impact.

The money supply has been expanded from MO_0 to MO_1 to offset the increase in transactions demand (from L_t to L_t'). The equilibrium rate of interest is the same, r^*, and so is the speculative demand for money, L_s. Remember that the money supply includes both currency and demand deposits. The actual increase in currency supplied need be only about 1/10 of the increase $MO_1 - MO_0$, depending upon cash reserve and cash drain ratios.

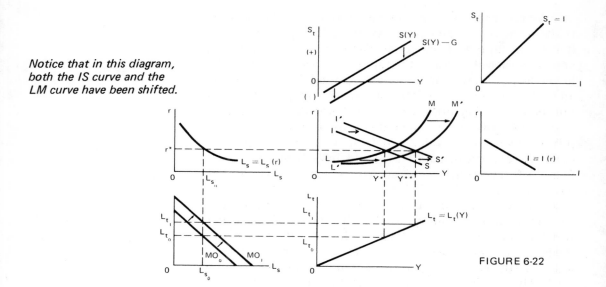

Notice that in this diagram, both the IS curve and the LM curve have been shifted.

FIGURE 6-22

Monetary Policy in the General Model

In order to make fiscal policy fully effective, we have seen that the government will have to undertake monetary policy to counter the rise in interest rates which would otherwise occur. Do similar problems arise with monetary policy? We can find the answer by shifting the money supply (the primary tool of monetary policy) and watching what happens. Figure 6-23 shows the shift in the money supply (an increase from MO_0 to MO_1) and the resulting effect on the LM curve.

Again, make sure you understand why one of the curves in our diagram has been shifted while the other has not.

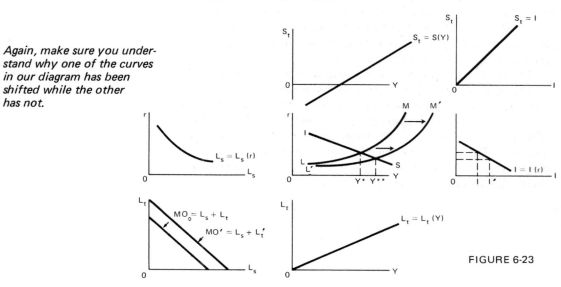

FIGURE 6-23

98

As long as the LM curve slopes upward to the right, the effect of an increase in the money supply can be seen to be a lowering of the rate of interest, a higher level of investment from the private sector, and an increase in aggregate income just large enough to provide the extra private savings needed to provide for the increased investment demand.

Keynes suggested, however, that in fact the LM curve could have a horizontal portion due to the liquidity trap (he was careful not to state flatly that it *did* have such a shape, only that it might). If that is indeed the case, then we can easily see that any expansionary monetary policy is completely useless, and the entire job of regulating aggregate demand rests on fiscal policy. Figure 6-24 shows what could happen to monetary policy under these conditions.

If you're unsure of the concept of a liquidity trap, check back to page 83 to make sure you understand how the problem might arise.

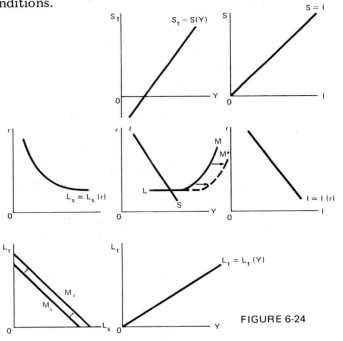

FIGURE 6-24

All that happens here is that because everyone believes that interest rates are going to rise, no one is willing to hold bonds. The government cannot drive down the rate of interest, and thus cannot increase private investment, so monetary policy can have no influence on aggregate demand. Monetary policy is ineffective, but over the horizontal section, fiscal policy is fully effective. By this we mean that an expansionary (or contractionary) fiscal policy will not raise (lower) the interest rate, and hence will leave private investment unaffected. Many people believe that this was the case during the great depression of the 1930s.

Appendix: Summary

1.   Fiscal policy operates by shifting the IS curve. Monetary policy operates by shifting the LM curve.
2.   Fiscal policy requires the shifting of either the "savings" function (by taxes or expenditure changes) or the investment function (by altering the expectations of businessmen).
3.   Monetary policy is undertaken by regulating the supply of money, normally via open market operations conducted by the central bank.
4.   Fully effective monetary and fiscal policy for stabilization may require the simultaneous changing of both policies to complement one another.

Appendix: Questions for Discussion

1.   What is the difference between the desire to invest (the demand for investment) and the desire to purchase bonds? Explain the relation between the desire to purchase bonds and the desire to hold money. Relate each of these to the desire to hold currency.

2.   What will happen to monetary policy if investment is interest-rate-inelastic? To fiscal policy?

3.   What will happen to monetary policy if we are in a liquidity trap? To fiscal policy?

4.   Assuming that we have neither a completely interest-rate-inelastic investment schedule nor a liquidity trap, explain why any fiscal policy the government undertakes will be in part self-limiting unless monetary policy is undertaken at the same time. (Hint: what will happen to the rate of interest due to fiscal policies?)

5.   Given that individuals wish to save one-tenth of their incomes; (mps = APS = 0.1 at all levels of income) investors wish to invest according to the following schedule:

$$\frac{10,000}{r-2};$$

the speculative demand for money is

$$\frac{5,000}{r-2};$$

the transactions demand for money is equal to .2Y; and the money supply is 25,000, solve for the equilibrium rate of interest, level of aggregate income, and level of investment. What level of government expenditure will be necessary to generate an income level of 200,000, assuming that the interest rate is to be maintained at the same level?

7

Monetary Policy in Canada

We have described the major Canadian monetary institutions (Bank of Canada, chartered banks, near banks, and the money market) and have outlined the main components of monetary theory. We are now in a position to show how monetary policy works in Canada. Remember that the purpose of monetary policy is twofold — first, to help, along with fiscal policy, to stabilize the economy; and second, to permit fiscal policy to be fully effective by accommodating the needs of fiscal measures. What we will deal with in this chapter is the institutional mechanisms which control monetary policy.

The Tools of Monetary Policy

As mentioned earlier, the Bank of Canada is the institution that implements government monetary policy. It has four recognized tools which it can use — moral suasion, the bank rate*, the variable liquidity ratio, and open market operations. We shall now look at these in turn.

Moral suasion is a rather difficult tool to describe adequately or to assess the importance of. What it means is that the officials of the Bank of Canada call together privately the officials of the chartered banks and "suggest" certain policies that the central bank thinks the commercial banks should follow, such as restricting consumer credit, buying government bonds, reducing advertising of loans. Moral suasion has no legal power although the chartered

Moral suasion has been used quite extensively in Canada, particularly since the Second World War. A couple of recent examples may illustrate. In 1965, after a major finance company failed, the Bank of Canada requested the chartered banks to make all necessary credit available to other finance companies to prevent any further failures. In 1968, after the United States introduced strict policies to improve its international balance of payments, policies which

*In the United States and some other countries, the bank rate is known as the discount or the rediscount rate.

101

largely exempted Canada, the Bank of Canada instructed Canadian banks and other financial institutions not to accomodate American corporations in providing services to evade the U. S. guidelines.

banks usually comply.* Discretion is the better part of valour.

The bank rate is the rate of interest charged on loans by the Bank of Canada to the chartered banks and certain other financial intermediaries. Why would the banks want to borrow from the Bank of Canada? Because they are required by law to maintain a legal cash reserve ratio. In Canada, the chartered banks must keep four per cent reserves against savings deposits and 12 per cent reserves against demand deposits. Since Canadians tend to keep around three-quarters of their deposits as savings deposits, the average legal reserve ratio has approximated 6½%. Should the cash reserves fall below this level, the banks would be obligated to borrow from the Bank of Canada to repair their reserves. The interest rate that they would be charged would be the bank rate. Thus, if the Bank of Canada raises this rate, it should discourage the chartered banks from loaning out fully. The banks would tend to follow a more conservative lending policy, raising their own interest rate on loans and possibly holding an extra cushion of reserves.

In fact in Canada, unlike in the U.S., the chartered banks have never made a regular practice of borrowing from the central bank. Thus, the bank rate has not had a significant effect via this mechanism. Rather, it has what is usually called a "signal" effect. That is, it has become largely the barometer of monetary policy. A barometer doesn't make weather — it tells what the weather is likely to be. The bank rate tells all of the banks, financial institutions and the public what the monetary climate will be. Therefore, it affects expectations and this alone can have important effects on the economy. (Canada's experience with the bank rate is recorded in Appendix Table 7-1.) For example, if the central bank raises the bank rate people may expect all interest rates to rise. They will wish to hold more of their assets as cash (and less in bonds) rather than risk a capital loss. Thus, the demand for money will rise and with it the interest rate, thereby cutting investment and helping to dampen the economy. This is just one way in which the bank rate, by "flying the colours", or publicising government intentions, can affect the economy.

Until recently Canada had a *variable cash reserve ratio.* This meant that the Bank of Canada had the legal power

*In the U.S. moral suasion is not used in quite the same way, presumably because of the difficulties of getting together the thousands of commercial bank officials. Instead the Federal Reserve uses what has been called an "open mouth policy" (as contrasted to open market policies). Speeches given by Reserve officials have somewhat the same suggestive effect as Canada's more discreet and genteel system.

to change the cash reserve ratio held by the banks between limits of 8 and 12%. To show how this would work consider a hypothetical banking system required to hold 8% reserves. The fully loaned out position is illustrated in the following table.

TABLE 7-1

Assets		Liabilities	
Cash Reserve	1 Million	Deposits	12.5 Million
Loans	11.5 Million		
Total	12.5 Million		12.5 Million

$$\text{Cash Reserve Ratio} = \frac{\text{Cash Reserves}}{\text{deposits}} = \frac{1}{12.5} = 8\%$$

Let us now assume that the central bank raises the requirement to a 10% reserve. With cash reserves of 1 million, total deposits must be reduced to 10 million. Therefore, the chartered banks will call in loans or not renew loans coming due until the situation is as shown below:

Try working out an example to show what would happen if the reserve ratio were raised to 12%. What would you expect to happen to the average interest rates banks would charge for loans?

TABLE 7-2

Assets		Liabilities	
Cash Reserve	1 Million	Deposits	10 Million
Loans	9 Million		
Total	10 Million		10 Million

In this example the money supply (deposits) has decreased by 2.5 million, or 20%. This would tend to raise interest rates, thereby reducing investment and aggregate demand as shown in the last chapter.

Changing the reserve ratio, however, is a very drastic and somewhat inflexible tool and was never used in Canada. As a result, it was replaced by the *variable liquidity ratio*. This means that the chartered banks as well as being required to hold fixed cash reserves, must also hold reserves of very liquid assets (near money) in the form of treasury bills. It is the liquidity ratio of cash plus treasury bills to deposits that now falls under the control of the Bank of Canada. The theoretical argument behind the liquidity ratio is too complex to deal with here. However, the effect of changing the liquidity ratio which the Bank of Canada can do (within the limits of from 0% to 12%) works so as to make monetary policy, whether restrictive or expansionary, more effective. These three tools are useful supports to monetary policy, but the most important and widely used tool is open market operations.

Open Market Operations

By far the most important tool of monetary policy in Canada is the buying and selling of bills and bonds in the money market by the Bank of Canada. These purchases and sales are together known as *open market operations.* Although moral suasion, bank rate manipulation, and adjustments in reserve requirements could be used, it is safe to say that open market operations have been and will remain the essential feature in regulating the monetary sector of the Canadian economy.

To see how open market operations work, we should remember that increasing the demand for a product (shifting its demand curve outward) normally has the effect of raising its price. This is what happens when the Bank of Canada decides to buy bonds or bills on the money market: the price of these securities tends to rise.

We saw earlier that changes in the rate of interest had a distinct effect on the price of a bond. The converse is also true. When the price of a bond is bid up, the effective rate of interest on that bond falls. This happens because the interest payment is a fixed number of dollars, and a higher price for the asset means a lower rate of return per dollar.

That is, when the Bank of Canada buys bonds on the open market, it is carrying on a policy of monetary ease, lowering the rate of interest, and hence stimulating investment and AD as we saw earlier. (See Appendix Table 5-1 for Canadian money supply levels.)

The Bank of Canada has the power to buy or sell a wide variety of financial instruments. In practice, however, the Bank usually restricts its activities to purchases and sales of Canadian government securities, and only deals with Canadian financial institutions and investment dealers. The Bank enters the market on a regular weekly basis, participating in a treasury bill auction, but it also frequently buys or sells Federal government securities on other occasions.

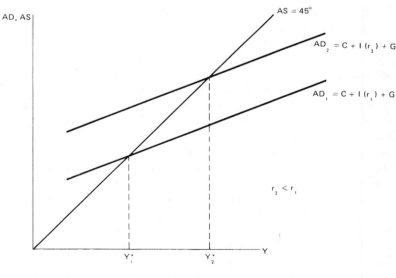

FIGURE 7-1

104

We can look at the effects of this policy in a way which fits in more closely with the discussion in Chapter 6. Figure 7-1 reproduces the diagram we used to show the way in which the equilibrium level of national income is affected by different rates of interest, working through changes in investment levels.

When the Bank of Canada buys bonds, it is trading a liquid asset (money) for a slightly less liquid asset (bonds or bills). Say the Bank of Canada pays cash for the bonds it buys. Now people who were holders of bonds are holding currency. If they decide to deposit some or all of that currency in the banking system, the cash reserves of banks are increased. This provides banks with a new supply of credit which they can extend to the public.* With an increased supply of credit, and the same demand schedule for credit as before, the price of credit, or the rate of interest, can be expected to fall.

The fact that there are these two ways of looking at the same operation has led economists to two different points of view. One school of thought argues that the supply of money is the critical variable in the conduct of monetary policy. The other claims that it is the rate of interest which is important. We do not need to worry too much about this difference of opinion because in our model the two are so closely connected, and it would not help us to get caught up in the old question about the chicken and the egg. We have so far accepted the claim that it is the rate of interest which really matters, and that the level of the money supply is simply one of the forces (along with the demand for money) which *determines* the rate of interest.

When the Bank of Canada decides to *sell* bonds on the open market, it must lower the price (and raise the rate of interest) in order to sell the increased supply on the market. That is, when the Bank sells a new bond issue, it is carrying out a restrictive monetary policy. Or, from another viewpoint, because it is trading less liquid for perfectly liquid assets, the central bank is running down individuals' or banks' reserves of currency, and thus is causing a contraction in the supply of credit (or money) available. This pushes the rate of interest up and reduces the equilibrium quantity of borrowing. AD is reduced.

To show just how the procedure works, let us consider an example where the Bank of Canada sells one million dollars worth of bonds to the public. Say the bonds are paid for by cheques drawn against accounts at the char-

*The maximum amount of the credit expansion (contraction) will be equal to the initial increase (decrease) in reserves times the money multiplier, $\frac{1}{\text{crr}}$.

We can illustrate the effects of monetary policy on a diagram which shows the demand for money as a function of the rate of interest and the level of income. If the monetary authority shifts the supply of money, (from M_0 to M_1) the rate of interest will fall, (to r_1 from r_0) other things remaining the same, as shown in figure i.

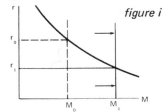
figure i

But we must note that things do not remain the same. The change in interest rates affects investment levels, which are part of AD, and thus change the equilibrium income level, as shown in figure ii.

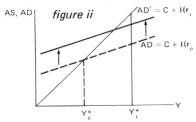
figure ii

The change in income levels shifts the demand for money schedule (since with a higher income, more money is needed for transactions purposes), so that the ultimate result is that shown in figure iii.

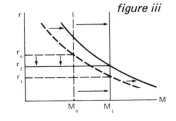
figure iii

---

tered banks. As part of its clearing-house function, the central bank then subtracts these cheques from the accounts which the chartered banks keep with the Bank of Canada as part of their reserves.

Before the transaction, the balance sheet of the chartered banks in the aggregate might look something like this:

TABLE 7-3

Assets			Liabilities	
		millions		millions
Cash Reserves: Vault Cash		2	Deposits:	100
Deposits in the Central Bank		8		
Loans: Direct Loans		80		
Treasury Bills		10		
Total:		100	Total:	100

Immediately after the sale of bonds, the chartered bank balance sheet would appear as follows:

TABLE 7-4

Assets			Liabilities	
		millions		millions
Cash Reserves: Vault Cash		2	Deposit:	99
Deposits in the Central Bank		7		
Direct Loans		80		
Treasury Bills		10		
Total:		99	Total:	99

But we can see from the lower account that the ratio of reserves (vault cash plus deposits with the central bank) has now fallen below the 10% level which was originally maintained, to 1/11 or 9.1%. Let us assume that the banks are legally required to hold 10% reserves. This means that after the bond sale, they will have to build up their vault cash, their deposits with the central bank, or both to 10% of their deposits, or 9.9 million. How will they do this? By calling in some of the loans they have made, or by selling some of their treasury bills. They will only stop doing so when they reach the situation shown below:

TABLE 7-5

Assets			Liabilities	
		millions		millions
Cash Reserves: Vault Cash		2	Deposits:	90
Deposits in the Central Bank		7		
Loans: Direct Loans		72		
Treasury Bills		9		
Total:		90	Total:	90

We cannot be sure just how much of the extra reserves will come from the sale of treasury bills, and how much will come from the loans which are called in, nor can we be sure how the banks will choose to hold reserves, so the numbers above for those quantities after the new equilibrium has been reached are simply to show what might happen.

We *can* be sure of one thing, however. That is that the supply of money and credit has been restricted. And to make the supply of money (or credit) equal to the demand once more, the rate of interest will have to rise. We can see from looking at the banks that this will be the case. Which loans will the banks try to call in first? Those with the lowest rates of interest. Which new loans will the banks be most likely to supply, if they supply any at all? Those with high rates of interest. This gives us another way of looking at the methods by which restrictive monetary policy drives up the price of credit and hence cuts down on the equilibrium quantity.

The Availability of Credit Doctrine

Up to now we have assumed that monetary policy works solely through the interest rate and its affect on investment. Thus, a decrease in money supply increases interest rates thereby decreasing investment and in turn aggregate demand. A rise in money supply (within previously mentioned limits) decreases interest rates, raising investment and hence aggregate demand. However, money is borrowed not only for investment, but also for consumption (consumer loans). Therefore, we might expect monetary policy to affect consumption demand as well as investment. The difficulty is, however, that studies have shown that consumers often either don't know or don't care about interest rates on consumer loans. (This is the same as making the assumption that we made in a previous chapter, that savings is not a function of the interest rate.)

Does this mean that consumption is unaffected by monetary policy? No. Consumers may or may not be deterred from borrowing when the interest rate goes up. But even if they may be willing to pay the higher interest cost they may find themselves unable to find credit. Similarly, individuals investing in housing may not be too concerned about their interest costs (within reasonable limits), but may also find themselves denied credit.

Basically, it is argued, the financial institutions ration credit out on some base other than its price. Take the

Government credit restrictions have not been widely used in North America except in wartime. In Britain, however, they have been used quite extensively. One popular device has been control of the percentage of the purchase price paid as down payments on credit purchases, (known in Britain

107

as hire-purchase agreements).
Thus, when the authorities
wish to dampen the economy,
they raise the required down
payment on such consumer
durables as cars, appliances,
motorcycles and televisions.
This tends to reduce the demand for these items and to
increase savings as people
attempt to accumulate the
required cash down payment.
In Canada, such methods
have been largely restricted
to down payments on housing
financed under the National
Housing Act.

example of Mr. Jones who has borrowed money in the past from his local bank to purchase a car, TV and several other appliances. He now wants to borrow to purchase a boat. But this time when he goes to the bank, the monetary authorities have restricted the money supply through open market operations and the banks are forced to reduce their outstanding loans. Mr. Jones may be able and willing to pay a higher interest rate on a loan to purchase his boat. Chances are, however, that the bank will turn him down and he will thus have to postpone his boat purchase. Thus, "tight money" will produce a decline in consumption as a result of credit restrictions rather than because of the change in interest rate. The same argument can be applied to explicit government policies of credit controls such as raising the minimum levels of down payments and similar instruments.

The most prominent example of credit rationing occurs in the housing (mortgage) market and affects investment in housing. For example, a man earning $5,000 per year wishes to build a new house for which he needs a mortgage of $13,000. Mortgage companies will normally only grant a mortgage where the monthly payments do not exceed 25% of the borrower's income. Therefore, as long as the house payments do not exceed $104 per month the man would be eligible to obtain a mortgage. At an interest rate of 8.5% his payments would be $103 (on a 25-year term), thus permitting our man to obtain his mortgage and build a house — thereby adding to aggregate demand. Now assume that the interest rate is raised by government policy to 9.5%. Monthly payments would now rise to $112. Since this is in excess of 25% of the income of our man, he would be unable to obtain a mortgage regardless of whether he is willing, and able, to pay the higher rate. Thus, again, a non-price rationing system has restricted credit and the effect on aggregate demand is the same as if the decision not to build had been made because of the higher price of credit.

The effect of rationing credit operates in the same direction as that produced by interest rate changes on investment although consumption as well as investment is involved. We could modify our previous theoretical model to reflect the doctrine of credit availability, but it would complicate the analysis without adding significantly to our understanding. Nevertheless, credit restrictions operating either through the operation of financial institutions or through conscious government policies should be considered as supplements to monetary policy in its effects on the economy.

Summary

1.   The Bank of Canada is responsible for implementing monetary policy. It has four major tools: moral suasion, the bank rate, the variable liquidity ratio and open market operations. The most important and often used of these is open market operations.

2.   The sale by the central bank of bonds on the open market tends to raise interest rates and contract the supply of money through the money multiplier process (a restrictive monetary policy). The purchase of bonds by the central bank operates in the opposite direction (an expansionary monetary policy).

3.   Because of institutional constraints in financial markets, monetary policy affects not only the *cost* of credit (interest rates) but also the *availability* of credit ("tight money" or "easy money").

Questions for Discussion

1.   Assume that the Bank of Canada, using moral suasion, asked the chartered banks to stop advertising designed to encourage people to take out consumer loans. What would be the probable effect?

2.   If the Bank of Canada announced that it was lowering the Bank Rate from 8½% to 8%, what would you expect the government was concerned with, inflation or unemployment? Why?

3.   What would be the effect of the government passing legislation requiring all purchasers of new cars to pay 50% of the selling price as a down payment? Under what economic conditions might this policy be used? What difficulties would you foresee?

4.   Assume that at the regular weekly auction of Government Treasury Bills, the Bank of Canada buys $2 millions worth. The government transfers this money to its accounts in the chartered banks. The following is the consolidated accounts of the chartered banks before the sale. The legal reserve ratio is 5%.

Assets		Liabilities	
Cash in vaults and reserves in B of C	50 million	Deposits	1,000 million
Outstanding loans	950 million		
Total Assets	1,000 million	Total Liabilities	1,000 million

If the banks proceed to become fully loaned out, show the resulting consolidated accounts of the chartered banks. What is the change in the money supply? What would you expect would happen, if anything, to interest rates?

8

The Keynesian Model with an International Sector

In preceding chapters we have made the assumption that our economic system is a closed economy. This is the economists' way of saying there is no international trade. In fact, of course, Canada's economy is a very open one. In 1968, for example, exports of goods and services represented over 25 per cent of gross national output. (By way of comparison, the comparable U.S. figure was approximately 6 per cent.) In order to make our theoretical model more realistic therefore, we must introduce the international sector. This will be done first in an economy where investment is autonomously determined and then in the more general model which was presented in Chapter 6, where investment was made a function of the rate of interest. Before dealing with our aggregate supply-demand model, we will briefly review the determinants of the existence and level of international trade.

The Basis of International Trade

The basic reasons for international trade are no different than the reasons for internal trade. Consider trade between Ontario and Quebec. Now assume that the separatists gain control, resulting in Quebec's secession. Unless artificial barriers are erected between the two provinces, there is no *economic* reason for a change in the trading situation. In other words interprovincial trade has become international trade merely because of the change in status of a political border.

Trade takes place because *specialization* promotes efficiency and lower costs. Hence a country will import goods which it can buy from a foreign country for less than it costs to produce them domestically. If it were to produce the goods itself, it would have to give up the production of a greater value of other goods in order to transfer the resources needed to replace those currently imported. No doubt Canada could produce bananas if it transferred capital, labour and other resources from some other industry to the building of heated greenhouses. The cost, however, would be very high. Similarly, we export goods that we can produce at a relatively lower cost than foreign countries. Presumably, foreign countries would be willing to buy Canadian goods as long as the price was less than it would cost them to produce the same goods. Thus each country tends to specialize in those goods where it has a *comparative* (or relative) advantage due to resource endowment, acquired skills, specialized knowledge or similar advantage. For this reason, trade will normally take place even if one country is more efficient in producing *all* goods. Each will still tend to specialize in what it does best relative to other countries.

Some aspects of the theory of comparative advantage have been critized by some economists but basically, most economists tend to support the freest international trade possible so that, with every country producing what it can do best, total world output will be maximized. This is why economists tend to oppose most forms of tariff protection and has been a major reason for recent international agreements to reduce tariffs. The combination of tariff reductions and post-Second World War economic development in many countries has resulted in a very rapid rate of growth in international trade. We will now show what effect trade has on aggregate demand.

against us, that we have every reason to believe that he has been excited to this course by our perfidious neighbour England . . . . In this belief we are confirmed by the fact that in all his transactions with that proud island, he is much more moderate and careful than with us."

International Trade and Aggregate Demand

Let us consider a simplified international trade model for two countries, Canada and Great Britain. This is a partial equilibrium model in that we will consider the rate of exchange between Canadian dollars and British pounds as fixed, as are all other variables. We will also assume that there are no tariffs or transport costs. Let us further assume that only wheat and automobiles are traded. The following four diagrams show the supply and demand situations in the two countries *without international trade*. Note that all prices are expressed in terms of Canadian dollars.

Much confusion has resulted from different countries naming their currencies the same even though there is no fixed connection between them. Thus Canada, the United States and Australia all have "dollars", a name with roots in German and Spanish currency. Other examples are

111

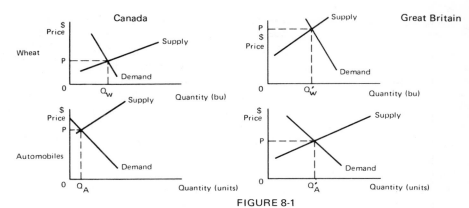

FIGURE 8-1

numerous countries originally in the British empire which use use the pound, or the Scandinavian countries which use the Kroner. The fact that the value of the Canadian and American dollars has been relatively close for historic reasons, has obscured the fact that they need have no tendency to parity. For the sake of students of economics, our currency would have been much better named the "Beaver", which would not only prevent the confusion in terminology and avoid the belief by many that the U.S. and Canadian currencies for some reason should have the same value, but also would be more historically relevant to the development of money in the Canadian economy.

Without trade, the price for wheat in Britain will be considerably above that in Canada. The reverse situation would exist for cars. With international trade, however, the prices will tend to equalize with Canada's exports of wheat being identically equal to Britain's imports of wheat and Britain's exports of cars being identically equal to Canada's imports of cars. This is shown in Figure 8-2.

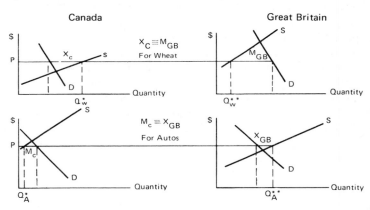

FIGURE 8-2

Canada's exports of wheat (X_C) have a value of X_C times the price of wheat. Therefore, our export demand is $X_C P_W$ (where P_W is the price of wheat). This is also the demand for imports to Britain. Similarly, Canada's import demand is the quantity of cars imported (M_C) times the price of cars, (P_A) or $M_C P_A$. We denote the value of Canadian exports as X and the value of Canadian imports as M. Note that there is no reason why exports and imports need be of equal value in this partial equilibrium situation.

While we have developed this model on the basis of two countries and two commodities, the extension to many countries and many commodities involves nothing new theoretically — just more diagrams.

112

Balance of Payments

Before proceeding to incorporate our X and M demands into the Keynesian model, we should look at the assumption we made in the previous section dealing with a fixed ratio of Canadian dollars to British pounds. Let us say, for instance, that 1 bushel of wheat costs $2.00 in Canada. The price in Britain will be quoted, not in dollars, but in pounds. If one pound is worth 2 dollars, then the price of wheat in Britain will be £1 per bushel. But if one pound is worth 3 dollars, then the price of wheat in Britain will be £2/3 per bushel. Since demand for Canadian wheat in Britain is a function of the British price, the ratio between the two currencies automatically affects the prices of our exports and imports. What then determines the ratios (or prices) of our moneys on the international market?

Basically, if there were no fixing of the price of one country's currency in terms of the currency of other countries (this price is the *exchange rate*), their relative values would be determined on the market by supply and demand like any other commodity. We then must look at what determines the demand for and supply of British and Canadian currencies on the market. We will be talking only in terms of the supply and demand for Canadian money to make things simpler.

The British, if they wish to buy Canadian goods, must pay for these goods in money that is acceptable in Canada: this means in Canadian dollars, which are the only legal money in Canada. Therefore, Canadian exports constitute a demand for $s. But this is not the only demand. Say a British bank wants to invest money in Canada either in long-term stocks or bonds or in short-term treasury bills or term deposits. It must again invest money that is acceptable in Canada, which means it must convert its British currency into $s. This constitutes a second demand for $s.

On the other side of the ledger, Canadians wishing to buy British goods have to convert their money into British money first by offering, or supplying, Canadian $s to the international market in exchange for the necessary foreign money. This is the first source of supply of Canadian dollars. Secondly, Canadians who wish to invest in Britain must first offer their dollars on the market in order to buy £s, which they can then invest in short or long-term loans or equities. This is also a supply of C$s on the market. We can now show in tabular form the supply and demand for $s on the international market. (See Appendix Table 8-1 for dollar values.)

TABLE 8-1

Demand for Canadian Dollars	Supply of Canadian Dollars
Current Account*	
Exports of merchandise	Imports of merchandise
Exports of services (travel, freight and shipping, interest and dividends, etc.)	Imports of services
Capital Account*	
Long-term capital imports (direct investment, long-term security borrowings)	Long-term capital exports
Short-term capital imports	Short-term capital exports

At any given level of prices and interest rates, therefore, we can draw up supply and demand schedules that would, in the absence of any government intervention, determine a price for Canadian dollars (expressed in terms of British pounds). (See Appendix Table 8-2 for a record of exchange rates.) Remember that as the exchange rate goes up (that means the Canadian dollar becomes more expensive and the £ becomes cheaper), Canadian goods will become more expensive in Britain. Normally this will result in a decline in the demand for Canadian goods in Britain and a rise in the demand for British goods in Canada. Let us take the following example. British demand for wheat is, at Canadian price, $2 bu.:

TABLE 8-2

Exchange Rate	Price	Quantity Demanded	Demand for $	Supply of £
1£ = 2$	1£	1 mill bu.	2 mill $	1 mill £
1£ = 3$	2/3 £	2 mill bu.	4 mill $	4/3 mill £

Let us assume that the demand for investment in Canada is $1 million. We can show the demand in the following Figure 8-3. Since the opposite reasoning holds for the supply of Canadian dollars, we can show supply and demand simultaneously to determine equilibrium price.

Where there is a *floating* exchange rate, that is, where the rate is determined only by supply and demand, the rate would be P_1. Since the Second World War most western countries have agreed not to allow their exchange rates to vary with supply and demand except for brief periods to allow them to find an equilibrium level. Under the terms which formed the International Monetary Fund (IMF), most nations have agreed to fix their exchange rates

*We refer to the table of imports and exports of goods and services as the current account; the table of flows of capital is known as the capital account.

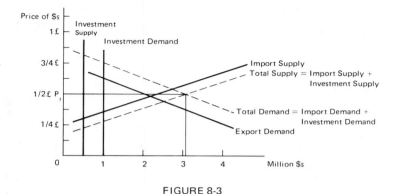

FIGURE 8-3

(with a small allowance for day-to-day fluctuations) primarily to provide a climate of stability for international trade and capital movements. Canada, however, operated on a freely floating rate from 1950 until 1962, when the rate was fixed. It was allowed to float again in mid-1970.*

How does the government maintain a fixed rate if supply and demand are not in equilibrium at the agreed rate? In fact, it is a simple matter if the true equilibrium is not too different from the agreed rate. The Bank of Canada, on behalf of the government, keeps a reserve fund of British and other foreign currencies (*foreign exchange fund*) which it uses to buy or sell foreign and Canadian currency on the market. Thus, if the demand for Canadian dollars is too low to maintain the agreed price, the fund buys dollars with its reserves of pounds or other currencies (mainly American dollars). If the supply of Canadian dollars is too low, the fund sells dollars in exchange for foreign currencies. In other words, the fund supplements supply or demand to control the price at the fixed exchange rate. With a floating rate, the Bank may still keep a foreign exchange fund to even out day-to-day variations.

If the supply of $s is greater than demand, the fund will buy $s. This is known as a *balance of payments deficit*. The fund can only continue until it runs out of foreign exchange reserves.** There is a *balance of payments surplus* if the demand for $s is greater than the supply at the fixed rate and the fund is selling Canadian dollars and building up reserves of foreign currency. Unlike the deficit situation, there is no physical limit to how high this fund could rise. However, political pressure from other

The amount of domestic money held in foreign countries is usually too small to have much of an effect on the domestic money supply, unless other countries regularly use your currency to pay off international debts to third countries. This has sometimes proven to be a problem for countries like Britain and the United States, but it has so far not affected Canada.

*The government has indicated that the exchange rate may be fixed again once it appears to have reached an equilibrium level.

**The fund can borrow foreign exchange up to agreed limits from the International Monetary Fund to cover an emergency situation. Sooner or later, however, these borrowings must be paid back.

countries normally will be felt because our surplus is their deficit. In any case, it does not make economic sense to continue building up idle reserves.

This foreign exchange fund is used to stabilize the market rate at the fixed rate through short run changes in supply or demand. If, however, the reason for the imbalance is long run — if the fund is persistently losing foreign reserves to the point where it is threatened with running out, or if the fund is persistently gaining excess reserves — then the only alternative if domestic policies are held constant would be to change the fixed price. If there is a persistent balance of payments surplus, then we would raise the exchange rate or *revalue*. If it was a persistent deficit in the balance of payments, we would lower the exchange rate or *devalue*. We will come back to this later.

The Keynesian Model with an International Sector

The aggregate supply of goods put on the market by the Canadian economy is still C + S + T. However, aggregate demand is supplemented by foreign demand (X), but lessened by that part of Canadian demand satisfied by goods produced in other countries (M). Therefore, the net addition to other forms of demand is the difference between the value of exports and imports (X − M), which will be positive if there is a balance of trade surplus, or negative if there is a balance of trade deficit. We can now write AD = C + I + G + (X − M). We will simplify our analysis by assuming that both exports and imports are independent of (do not vary with) the level of NNP in Canada. In a case where M exceeds X, our equilibrium level of national income can be represented in the following diagram. As shown in Figure 8-4, equilibrium occurs where I + G + (X − M) = S + T. (This is sometimes expressed I + G + X = S + T + M.)

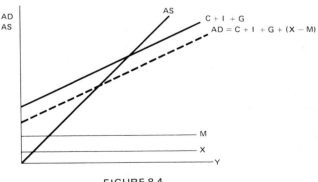

FIGURE 8-4

During the latter half of 1971, the United States, worried about its exchange position (and perhaps about a short-run loss of jobs to foreign imports in the year leading up to a presidential election?) began putting considerable pressure on its trading partners, including Canada, which was on a flexible rate, to adjust their exchange rates upward in order to make U.S. goods cheaper abroad, and foreign goods more expensive in the U.S.

Canadian exports are highly concentrated in terms of destination. In recent years over two thirds of exports have gone to the United States. On a regional basis, Canadian exports are also very specialized. Thus, central Canada dominates in the export of manufactured goods, led by automobiles and automobile parts under the automotive trade agreement with the United States; the Prairies leads in exports of grain, chiefly wheat, and of oil; while B.C. and the northern areas of Quebec and Ontario predominate in

We can now relax our assumption that imports do not vary with income. It is reasonable to suppose that, since consumption rises as income rises and many of the goods we consume are imported goods, then imports will also tend to rise as NNP increases. In fact, in Canada imports appear to be quite sensitive to changes in income. On the other hand, there is no similar reason why exports should vary with Canadian income. The demand in other countries for Canada's exports is determined by conditions in those countries and price. As long as we hold prices constant (both domestic prices and exchange rates), then exports should remain constant.

The effect of an increase in imports as NNP rises is the same as that of taxes — they operate as a form of automatic stabilizer, draining off additional AD on Canadian resources as incomes rise and draining off less AD as incomes fall. We can represent the relationship between imports and income in the same way that we have with consumption, savings taxes etc. The proportion of new income that is spent on imports is the marginal propensity to import (mpm). Therefore, $M = M_0 + mpm \times NNP$. We can show this graphically in the following diagrams. Figure 8-5 shows the effect on AD. Figure 8-6 shows the equilibrium condition where $I + G + (X - M) = S + T$. (T and I are considered independent of income.) We can also show that in this case the multiplier is

$$k = \frac{1}{mps + mpm}.$$

mineral exports and, with the Maritimes, in pulp and paper. Changes in American demand for specific exports, therefore, can have important regional effects.

There is a fairly direct relationship between foreign investment, exports, and imports in Canada. A strong United States demand for primary goods, particularly minerals, has led to waves of foreign investment in this sector, thus giving impetus to aggregate demand and imports into Canada. Much foreign investment, furthermore, has come directly in the form of capital goods, thus increasing Canadian imports and dampening the expansive effect of foreign investment.

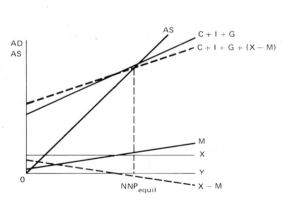

FIGURE 8-5

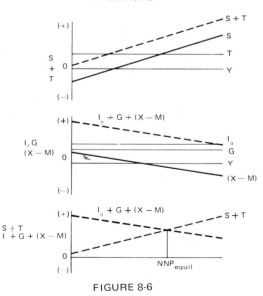

FIGURE 8-6

117

Commercial Policy

The ten per cent import "surcharge" imposed by President Nixon in August of 1971 on goods imported into the United States, and the consequent slackening of demand for Canadian goods in the U.S., illustrates just how vulnerable the Canadian economy can be. (The "surcharge", of course, was not really a surcharge at all, which would be an import duty imposed as a per cent of present levels of duty, but a direct 10 per cent tax on the value of the goods imported.)

Almost all countries raised tariffs drastically in the early 1930s. For instance, Canada between 1923 and 1933 raised its average tariff level approximately 50%. In part this was in retaliation to the increase in U.S. protection with the Smoot-Hawley (the names of the American legislators who introduced the tariff bill) tariffs of 1930 which raised the already relatively high U.S. rates by around 20%.

Previously we have shown how governments can influence the level of domestic output and employment by fiscal and monetary policies designed to influence various components of AD and thereby the equilibrium levels of income. The introduction of an international sector provides one additional area where discretionary policies could, in theory, be used to affect aggregate demand and thus the level of national income. We will refer to policies dealing with the international sector as *commercial policy*. The two major tools that could be used are altering (1) tariffs or (2) the exchange rate. Let us be clear, however, that use of these tools for stabilization purposes is rare since governments through international agreements such as the General Agreement on Tariffs and Trade (GATT) and the IMF are committed to using other policies (fiscal and monetary) for stabilization purposes except in certain emergency circumstances.

Let us deal with tariffs first. The effect of tariffs is to add a tax to imported goods so that they become more expensive for Canadian consumers or investors. This would normally encourage Canadians to buy fewer imported goods and more Canadian-produced goods than would otherwise be the case. In the case of unemployment in Canada, the government might be tempted to raise tariffs with the intention of decreasing imports. This would normally result in a rise in AD since — exports remaining constant and imports falling — our AD curve would shift upwards. In reality, however, other countries would be likely to retaliate by raising their tariffs and thus reducing our exports. Since we now have additional taxes (tariffs) and a decline in exports, we could very well be less well off than previously. This in fact happened during the great depression of the 1930s.

Lowering tariffs during periods of inflation, however, would increase imports, thereby lowering AD without much probability of retaliation. In practice this is not usually done because once the tariff is reduced, there is little possibility of reversal and tariffs can only be reduced to zero. In other words, it is a one shot affair.

The alteration in the official fixed exchange rate is a more useful tool of discretionary policy. Governments may devalue or revalue, not for stabilization purposes, but to solve balance of payments problems.

However, exchange rate policy has been used to reconcile domestic policies with export and import demands in order to prevent unemployment and inflation. Let us consider a situation of unemployment equilibrium. The government might initiate an expansionary fiscal policy and an easy monetary policy (low interest rates). These, however, might lead to difficulties if foreign lenders withdraw their savings* due to the low interest rates or if the expansion pulls in a large amount of new imports which lowers the multiplier effect of government policy. The government might have to run continuous budget deficits in order to achieve full employment. The alternative would be to devalue. This means that the Canadian dollars would decline in value relative to the currencies of other countries. Exports from Canada would become cheaper in price and imports into Canada would become more expensive. Presumably, therefore, Canadian exports would rise and foreign imports would fall and be replaced by domestically-produced goods. When we look at AD this means that $X\uparrow$ and $M\downarrow$ so that $(X - M)$ would rise significantly. All other things being equal, income and employment would rise to a new equilibrium level. Thus, assuming no retaliation, Canada could "export its unemployment" (which could, of course, cure someone else's inflation).

Similarly, if Canada was experiencing inflation which it could not or did not want to combat through restrictive monetary and fiscal policies, it might revalue, raising the price of the Canadian dollar thereby making imports cheaper and exports more expensive. All other things being equal, exports would decline and imports rise thereby lowering aggregate demand and "exporting inflation" (or perhaps helping to counteract a recession in other countries from whom we import).

In practice, devaluation and revaluation are not used for stabilization purposes. Rather, they are used to combat persistent deficits or surpluses in the balance of payments. Let us take an example. If Canada had undergone a long period of inflation, it is likely that she would find it difficult to export as much because of the rising prices and she would find herself importing more of the cheaper foreign goods. As a result, the supply of Canadian $s on the world market would rise and the demand for $s would fall. At the fixed exchange rate, therefore, there would be a deficit in the balance of payments (Supply > Demand). To solve this problem, the government could use restrictive monetary and fiscal policy hoping to produce enough unemployment to dampen imports and lower export prices. For political and economic reasons, no government will be anxious to do this and may devalue (i.e., reduce the ex-

*This is what we really mean when we talk about foreigners pulling out their "investments".

change rate) in order to raise exports and lower imports without having to resort to deflationary fiscal and monetary policies.

The very large proportion of the Canadian economy that is involved in international trade poses particularly serious problems for stabilization policies in Canada. This is due to the fact that Canada has little control over a very significant part of aggregate demand, in particular exports which are sensitive to policies and economic conditions in foreign countries. A recession in countries which buy Canadian goods, the imposition of tariffs or quotas against Canadian exports, or a devaluation of a foreign currency would have a significant effect in reducing aggregate demand in Canada. Any attempt to counter this decrease with fiscal policy (government spending, tax decreases) could produce a balance of payments problem (deficit). For this reason, many Canadian economists have argued that the Canadian exchange rate should not be fixed but should be free to find its own market price. Then the government could implement the appropriate fiscal or monetary policy without having to worry about the balance of payments. The exchange rate would automatically adjust to equate supply and demand. With fixed exchange rates, Canadian policy makers must always be concerned with the effect of domestic policy on its international position.

Canada, which exports approximately 25 per cent of its GNP, is obviously much more open an economy than the United States, for example, where the comparable figure is only about 5 per cent. In general, the larger a country's economy, the smaller will be the proportion of its economy devoted to trade, since many of the advantages of specialization will be available through interregional trade within the country itself. Britain's decision to join the Common Market can be seen in large part as the attempt of a relatively open economy to break down trade barriers and convert international trade into interregional trade within Europe as a whole.

Summary

1.   International trade (like internal trade) occurs because, due to natural or acquired resources, one producer or country has a cost advantage over others in the production of a good. By each specializing in what it does relatively best, total output will be highest. Countries will normally export those goods where they have a comparative (relative) cost advantage.

2.   On the international exchange market, foreigners will demand Canadian dollars to purchase exports from Canada. Canadians will supply dollars in order to purchase foreign currency to finance imports from these countries. Similarly, foreigners will demand Canadian dollars to finance investment in Canada, while Canadians will sell dollars to get foreign currency to invest abroad.

3.   The supply and demand for Canadian dollars will, under a floating exchange rate, determine the international price (exchange rate) of the Canadian dollar. If the exchange rate is fixed by government agreement, the Canadian Foreign Exchange Fund will supplement supply or demand to maintain the market rate at that fixed rate.

4.   The balance of payments measures the excess of supply (a deficit) or of demand (a surplus) under a fixed rate system. Short-term disequilibrium can be offset through the exchange fund operations. A fundamental or long-term disequilibrium requires either the use of domestic policies to alter exports, imports and/or

capital flows, or it requires a change in the fixed value of the dollar through devaluation or revaluation.

5.   Exports add to aggregate demand for Canadian output; imports subtract from aggregate demand in Canada. The net contribution of the foreign sector to aggregate demand, therefore, is X — M (exports minus imports).

6.   Commercial policy, involving government control of tariffs and the exchange rate, normally plays only a minor role in stabilization policy.

Questions for Discussion

1.   If international trade is supposed to occur because a country has a comparative cost advantage, why is it that Canada sells oil to the United States but at the same time buys oil from South America?

2.   An oft heard defence of tariffs is that it protects Canadian workers from low paid workers in foreign countries and thus makes for "fairer" competition. Discuss the validity of this argument.

3.   List all of the arguments for and against fixed versus flexible exchange rates. Which do you favour? Why?

4.   Assume oil is found in the North West Territories and that this results in a rush of foreign investment into Canada. What would you expect to happen to Canada's exchange rate and/or the foreign exchange fund under

(a)   a floating or flexible rate

(b)   a pegged rate.

5.   Assume Canada is at full employment. After recognizing Mainland China, exports to that country rose significantly while imports remained the same. What would happen in Canada to prices, employment, and exchange reserves if:

(a)   the country was on a fixed exchange rate? What policies might the government resort to in order to correct any problems that might result?

(b)   the country was on a floating exchange rate? Again, what corrective policies might be attempted?

6.   "As long as we do so much trade with the U.S. and have significant inflows of U.S. capital, Canada has little control over its national income and employment". Discuss.

APPENDIX: The Complete Keynesian Model

If you thought the Appendix to Chapter 6 looked complicated, brace yourself for this one! Again, it's really not nearly as difficult as it looks at first glance. And, believe it or not, this is the easiest way of putting the pieces together.

In Chapter 6 we looked at the general Keynesian model, but we assumed away completely the existence of countries other than Canada. In the first part of this chapter, we relaxed the assumption that the rest of the world did not exist, but we went back to our partial equilibrium model and largely ignored the monetary side of the economy. In this section we will introduce the monetary sector into the open economy by expanding upon the diagrammatic treatment of Chapter 6.

We have been dealing with an economy which could be divided into two basic sectors: the real sector, and the monetary sector, and we illustrated what we argued were the important relationships in each of the two. We will now add on a third sector, the external sector, which allows us to deal with imports and exports and international flows of capital. (We will have more to say about just what this international capital flow is shortly.)

Changes in the Real Sector: the IS Curve in an Open Economy

We have already pointed out that in dealing with AD, imports are equivalent to a leakage out of the circular flow of income, while exports are additions to that flow. When we draw the savings function for an open economy, we want to include the net effect of flows of imports and exports. That is, we add imports, M, to our savings function, and subtract exports, X, from that function.* Figure 8-7 shows the new "savings" function (S_w). We assume that imports are related to income (by means of the marginal propensity to import), while exports are autonomous.** These are the same assumptions we made in the earlier part of this chapter, so we will not say anything more about them here. What we should note at this point is that any change in propensities to import or in demand for our exports will affect the IS curve. An increase in demand for imports by Canadians, for example, would shift the Canadian $S + M - X$ function upward (that is, it would have the same effect as an increased desire to save by Canadians). An increase in

---

*As we have shown previously, the equilibrium condition is $I + (X - M) = S$ (or with government added $I + (X - M) = S_t$). We are merely adopting the form $I = S_t + (M - X) = S_w$ for simplicity.

**This of course means that we are back to a partial equilibrium model, though it is a much more comprehensive one than we first dealt with in Chapter 3.

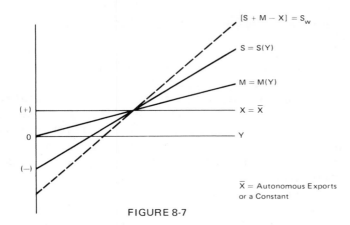

FIGURE 8-7

$\bar{X}$ = Autonomous Exports
or a Constant

demand for exports would shift the curve downward.

If we trace the effect of these on our new IS curve ("new" because it is now drawn for an open economy), we can see that with a fixed LM schedule, increased import demand leads to a lower equilibrium level of income (Figure 8-8), while increased exports leads to a higher equilibrium income level for the economy (Figure 8-9).

As far as the real sector alone is concerned, we can think of the effects of imports and the effects of savings together, and of exports and consumption demand as having similar effects. But this discussion provides us with only a part of the total picture. What, if any, are the effects of trade on the *monetary* sector? What of flows of *capital* between countries? These are questions we can answer with the help of another set of diagrams illustrating the international sector.

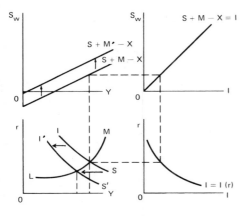

FIGURE 8-8

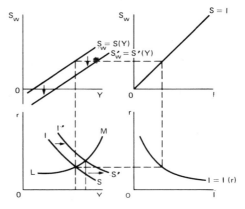

FIGURE 8-9

123

Trade and the Monetary Sector

Before we go on to talk about the international sector, we should see how (if) we need to alter the monetary sector of our model in any way to take account of trade. In fact, we do not need any such changes. Goods purchased from other countries must ultimately be paid for in the currency of those countries, and there is little reason for large quantities of money to be held for either transactions or speculative purposes (with the exception of speculation against future changes in the official exchange rate, at least). Some money might be held as part of other nations' foreign exchange reserves, of course.

This means that there need be no basic change in the liquidity preference schedule in the open economy (L_s), nor is there any increased demand to hold money for transactions purposes (L_t). As a result, we have exactly the same LM curve which we developed in Chapter 6. Figure 8-10 shows the development of the LM curve for the open economy.

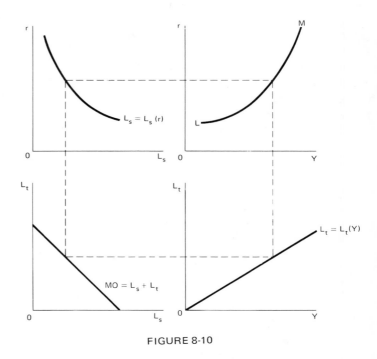

FIGURE 8-10

The International Sector

As was the case in the real and monetary sectors of the model, the basic relationships in the international sector can be illustrated by three graphs, each showing one relationship. We need one to show the flows of goods and services to and from our home country in the form of imports and exports; one to show the flows of capital (credit) to and from Canada; and a third which describes equilibrium in the international sector, which requires that any net inflow (outflow) of goods and services must be balanced by an outflow (inflow) of capital to finance that difference.

The Balance of Trade

The first of our three relationships involves the relationship of imports and exports to the level of national income in the home economy. We have argued that imports are related to the level of income through the propensity to import, so that imports as a function of aggregate income can be shown as in Figure 8-11. We are assuming that the exchange rate is fixed when we draw this relationship. We will relax that assumption and see what happens a little later.

Try not to confuse the balance of trade with the balance of payments. The former refers only to imports and exports of goods and services; the latter includes financial flows. For some reason, they are easy to mix up.

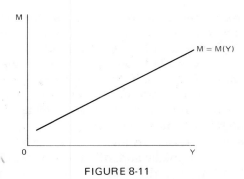

FIGURE 8-11

Exports are autonomous with respect to the level of Canadian income, as shown in Figure 8-12.

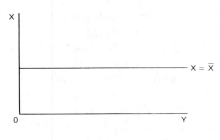

FIGURE 8-12

125

The sum of imports and exports together is shown in Figure 8-13 and it is this relationship we wish to use. The axis we use is called the *balance of trade*. It is simply the sum of the two, considering exports as a positive value (exports add to aggregate demand) and imports as a negative value (imports are a leakage out of the circular flow of domestic incomes and demand). At low levels of domestic income, imports will be low, and the balance of trade will be

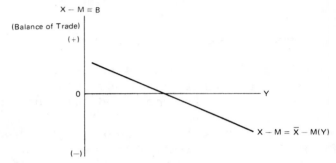

FIGURE 8-13

positive. As aggregate income rises, imports will rise. Exports remain the same because we hold (1) conditions in the rest of the world and (2) exchange rates constant. That is, the balance of trade is positive at low levels of income, and becomes negative as aggregate income increases. Just what the balance of trade curve looks like aside from this we cannot say. We drew it in Figure 8-13 as a straight line just to illustrate one possible shape.

The second relationship involves the flow of capital (or credit) between Canada and other countries. We will assume that when an individual makes the decision to purchase a bond or some other type of security, he looks not only at the level of domestic interest rates and bond prices, but also at those in the "rest of the world". If interest rates are higher in Canada than in other countries, then we will predict that Canadian bonds will be sold to individuals abroad. The higher are Canadian interest rates relative to those in the rest of the world, the higher will be the demand for Canadian bonds. Conversely, when Canadian interest rates are lower than those abroad, Canadian savings will flow abroad. The lower are Canadian rates relative to the rest of the world, the higher will be the demand in Canada for foreign bonds.

Because we are assuming that other things remain equal, one of which is the state of the world other than in the country we are dealing with, we assume that interest rates

126

abroad remain constant. This permits us to draw up a schedule showing the net quantities of capital flows to or from Canada at different levels of the Canadian interest rate. Figure 8-14 shows the relationship.

Capital flows are only in part determined by relative interest rates. Short-term capital movements are the most responsive to interest rates, but longer term capital movements into Canada are heavily influenced by patterns of foreign direct investment. For example, the demands of American industries for minerals and fuels has led to a heavy inflow of long term capital into Canadian resource development. Such an inflow of international investment would shift the capital flow curve in Figure 8-14 downwards.

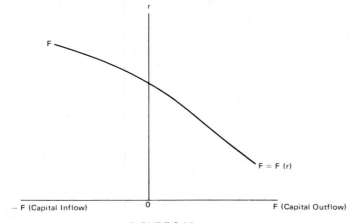

FIGURE 8-14

Note that we have the capital *outflow* on the horizontal axis. Values to the left of the vertical axis are read as negative capital outflows, or capital *inflow*. Figure 8-14 thus shows that when the Canadian rate of interest is high, we receive a capital inflow; if it is low, we incur a capital outflow.

The third and final relationship in the international sector involves the relationship which must hold if we are to have equilibrium in the sector. That is, the value of capital outflow from Canada must just equal the value of the surplus on current account (that is, the balance of trade), or the capital inflow to Canada must just equal

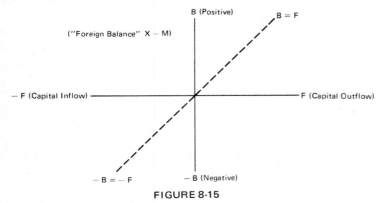

FIGURE 8-15

Canada's deficit on current account. Why is this necessary? Because if the two were not equal, the foreign exchange fund would be run down (if the deficit on current account

127

exceeded net capital inflow) or built up (if the net capital inflow is greater than the deficit on current account) under a fixed exchange rate, or there would be a change in the exchange rate if it were freely floating. In either event, we would not be in an equilibrium situation. Figure 8-15 shows the equilibrium relationship. This diagram is very similar to the one we used to show the equilibrium of savings and investment in the real sector, but it extends past the origin into the range where the balance on current account and the level of capital outflow are both negative.

We now have the three relationships we need to complete the international sector and our model of an open economy. Figure 8-16 shows how the three relationships fit together diagrammatically. We once more have three relationships, and four unknowns, so the result turns out to be not *a* position of equilibrium, but a set of equilibrium points once more.*

The fact that these diagrams have negative values for some of the flows shouldn't pose any difficulties, but they do look a little messy. Just remember that the value of (X − M) will be negative if imports exceed exports, while capital flows are negative when inflows exceed outflows.

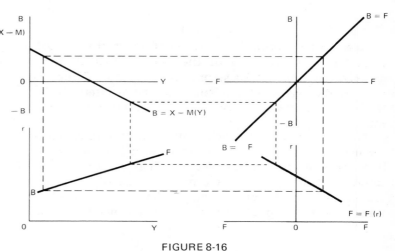

FIGURE 8-16

For each rate of interest, there is a level of income for which capital flows balance trade flows. The curve which shows this relationship (in Figure 8-16) is known as the BF curve.

The Complete Model

Now that we have dealt with each of the three sectors separately, it is time to fit them all together in a single

*The equations are

$$(1) \quad B = B(Y)$$
$$(2) \quad F = F(r)$$
$$(3) \quad B = F$$

where $B = X - M$, F is the level of capital outflow, and the solution is $B(Y) = F(r)$, one equation in two unknowns.

model, and to see just what effect adding the international sector will have on the conclusions we reached with the Hicks-Hansen model, the closed economy case. As was the case when we added the monetary sector to our first simple examination of AD and government fiscal policy, we will find that our policies may have to be shifted slightly. For one thing, this presentation should make clear the effects of fixed versus flexible exchange rates, and show plainly why economists almost invariably prefer the floating (free) rate.

Although we do not have room to show the derivation of the IS, LM, and BF curves all on the same diagram, each of the equilibrium relationships is shown for interest rates and incomes. Figure 8-17 shows one possible set of relationships, taking the LM curve as we derived it in Chapter 6 and adding to it the new IS curve and the international sector. To get both the IS and BF curve relationships on the diagram, we have put the IS curve derivation down in the lower left-hand corner, but there is no difference in the result.

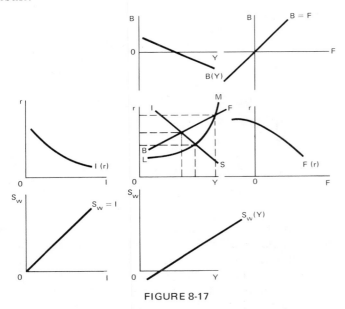

FIGURE 8-17

In the diagram above, we should note that there are three points for which two of the markets are in equilibrium, but nowhere are all three in equilibrium at the same combinations of income and interest rate. We said earlier that we could not be sure that the system would reach a general equilibrium at the full employment level of income. Now we cannot even be sure that it will reach *an* equilibrium at all!

If you're not quite sure how the model works at this point, have one more look at the discussion on the last few pages and then try tracing out the following discussion of policy. Seeing how the model works to help our analysis of government policy should help you to understand it.

Actually, this is a slight exaggeration because, if the exchange rate is a flexible (floating) one, the BF and IS curves will shift until some equilibrium is reached, although we cannot say just where that equilibrium will be.

To understand the complete model's workings, and to see just when and why the various curves will shift, let us consider a hypothetical case. Figure 8-18 shows the starting point. The full employment level of income is Y^{fe}, so that none of our three combinations of equilibrium are at sufficiently high levels to ensure full employment, even if we did get to one of them. Assume that the government wishes to ensure that there is full employment. What can the fiscal and monetary authorities do to get the economy there if they cannot use the exchange rate or any other commercial policy to regulate domestic conditions?

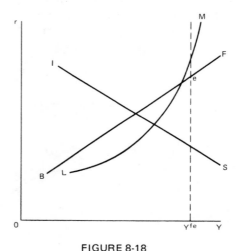

FIGURE 8-18

To achieve full employment under these conditions, there is only one possibility. General equilibrium will be where the BF curve (representing equilibrium in the international market) cuts the full employment line, at point e in Figure 8-18. This is because the BF curve is fixed (because the exchange rate is fixed), and we have to satisfy the condition that income be at the level Y^{fe} while the international sector is in equilibrium. Point e is the only situation where that occurs.

Now that we know where a general full employment equilibrium will be, how do the authorities make sure the economy reaches that point? They will obviously have to shift the IS and LM curves so that they both pass through point e, as shown in Figure 8-19.

130

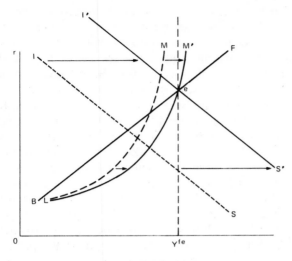

FIGURE 8-19

Remember that the government can shift the IS curve through fiscal policy. In this case, it wants to carry out an expansionary fiscal policy (run a deficit or a smaller surplus). At the same time, it should carry out an expansionary monetary policy (increase the supply of money) to shift the LM curve to the right. (Try drawing in all of the graphs for the real and monetary sector to see how much the expansion would have to be in each case.)

Starting from the position shown in Figure 8-18, it looks as if the government should not have too much difficulty getting the economy to full employment, but that might not always be the case. If the LM curve had a horizontal segment, as shown in Figure 8-20, then expansionary fiscal policy is needed to shift the IS curve to I'S', but contractionary monetary policy on a very large scale will be necessary to shift the LM curve to the left to L'M'.

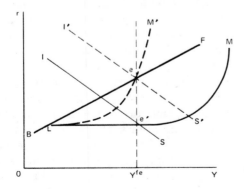

FIGURE 8-20

The authorities can still achieve full employment for the economy, but at a higher interest rate and with a lower level of investment than could be achieved if there were not the international sector to worry about. If the BF curve could be regulated like the IS and LM curves, then we could reach full employment equilibrium at point e', for example. Why might we prefer point e'? Well, for one thing, it involves a lower rate of interest, and a lower level of capital inflow (and of course a higher level of private investment). For a country like Canada, which has been worrying about foreign ownership and maintaining an adequate growth rate, it might be desirable to have a lower level of inflow (or even a capital outflow) without sacrificing investment because what that inflow consists of is purchases of Canadian stocks and bonds. Or, on the other hand, since high interest rates hit particular parts of the Canadian economy particularly hard (for example, the housing market), it may be undesirable for the government to follow a high interest-rate policy. We will have more to say about these "side effects" of macro policy in Chapter 10, including the problems of following an aggregative policy in an economy made up of a number of distinct regions.

Fiscal and Monetary Policy with a Flexible Exchange Rate

Although it is not usually possible for countries to use exchange rate adjustments or commercial policy to regulate the domestic economy because of a variety of international agreements, a country could allow its exchange rate to adjust freely, as Canada did from 1950 to 1962, and has recently permitted, in response to the forces of supply and demand in the international markets for Canadian currency. Businessmen and central bankers generally do not like flexible exchange rates very much because of the uncertainty about exactly how much one currency will be worth in terms of another at a particular point in time, but most economists favour them because of the additional power given to fiscal and monetary policies.

Remember that the exchange rate is the price of one currency in terms of another. Fixing that exchange rate is just like fixing any other price, whether it is the price of gin or the price of an hour's worth of labour (the wage rate). Unless the fixed rate is very near the actual free market rate, excess supply or excess demand will develop. Where currency is concerned, that means that international reserves will either be built up or run down if there is a difference between the market rate and the fixed rate.

Let us see what happens if we free the exchange rate, starting with the same situation we had in Figure 8-18. Let us say that the government selects a particular rate of interest r* it wishes to see as well as the full employment level of income. Can it achieve these two goals at the same time? It could not do so with the fixed rate of exchange. Figure 8-21 shows the first step in the process — a combi-

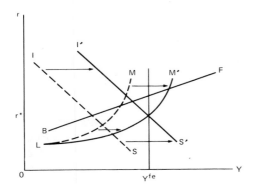

FIGURE 8-21

Make sure once again that you're clear on shifts in the curves versus movements along the schedules. In Figure 8-21, the IS and LM curves have shifted, while the BF curve has not.

nation of fiscal and monetary policies which achieve equilibrium in the domestic economy at the desired interest rate and income level. But at this point, the international sector is not in equilibrium. For that level of income, the rate of interest chosen is too low to provide for the capital inflow to finance the excess of imports over exports. Thus, the demand for foreign currency (for imports) is greater than the supply of foreign currency (from exports), and with a free market for currencies, the price of the foreign currency in Canadian dollars will be bid up.

Because foreign currency will then buy more Canadian dollars, we can expect foreigners to buy more Canadian goods and, because Canadian dollars buy less foreign currency than before, Canadians will buy fewer imported goods. Let us go back to the complete set of diagrams to see how this will affect the BF curve (Figure 8-22). With higher exports and lower imports, the relationship of the balance of trade to income will shift up and to the right, which has the effect of shifting the BF curve down and to the right, to B'F'. The graph showing capital flows will not change because, whatever the currency value, the *rate* of return will not change.

The BF curve will continue to shift until it reaches the point where the IS and LM curves cross, because only there will the income level be sufficient to ensure that the surplus or deficit on current account equals the deficit or surplus on the capital account.

133

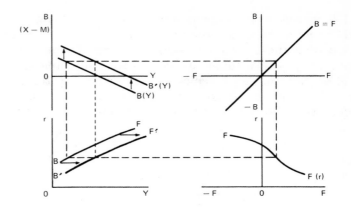

FIGURE 8-22

This is not quite the whole story, however. Our "new" IS curve also includes imports and exports, and we have just seen that these quantities are changing as a result of the change in the exchange rate. Figure 8-23 shows the

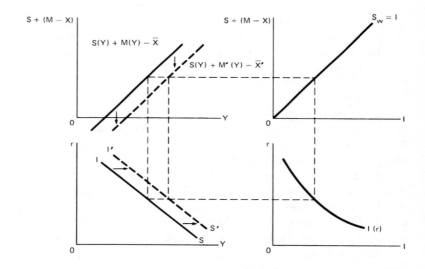

FIGURE 8-23

shift in the IS curve due to higher exports and lower imports.

We don't need to go into this problem in detail, but we might note that the government simply need not run as large a deficit because of the expansion in demand for Canadian goods by other countries and the reduction in demand for foreign goods by Canadians as it would have to do in a closed economy.

134

The actual policy undertaken is shown in Figure 8-24, where the shift in the IS curve is broken down into two parts: one a result of government fiscal policy; the other, a

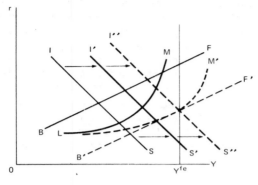

FIGURE 8-24

result of changes in the exchange rate.

This is as far as we will take our look at the complete open model, but it should serve to give an idea of the problems of policy in an open economy like Canada's and the way in which we might be able to solve them. One thing which is shown quite plainly by the model is the beneficial result which we get from having a flexible exchange rate. Leaving the exchange rate free permits the fiscal and monetary authorities to go about their business of ensuring full employment without having to worry about a potential balance of trade surplus or deficit. That may not sound like much, but most economists think that it is important enough to favour flexible exchange rates.

Appendix: Summary

1.   For equilibrium in the complete Keynesian system (in an open economy), there must be equilibrium not only in the goods market $(I + G + X - M = S + T)$ as represented by the IS curve and in the money market $(L_s + L_t = MO)$ as represented by the LM curve, but also in the foreign exchange market (external demand for Canadian dollars equal to supply of Canadian dollars to foreigners at the existing exchange rate) as represented by the BF curve.
2.   With flexible exchange rates, the BF and IS curves will automatically shift to produce an equilibrium level of national income, but that level may or may not produce full employment.
3.   If the exchange rate is fixed, the economy may not reach an equilibrium level of national income.
4.   Coordinated fiscal, monetary and commercial policies may be needed to produce equilibrium at the desired level of national income. This is particularly likely if either (a) the exchange rate is not flexible, or (b) the goal of a desired level of the rate of interest is combined with the goal of a particular national income level.

Appendix : Questions for Discussion

1.   Economists usually are in favour of flexible exchange rates. Bankers, particularly central bank officials, usually oppose them. Discuss the probable reasons behind these opposing views.

2.   *Canadian Businessman:* "The Canadian government should fix the value of the Canadian dollar at about ninety cents in U.S. currency. That way Canadian businessmen will be able to sell their products in the United States, and that will stimulate demand in Canada as well as give us a favourable balance of payments."

Snow shoveller: "Nonsense! If the Canadian dollar were worth only ninety cents U.S., I wouldn't be able to afford my Florida vacation this year. The government would do much better by setting the dollar at around $1.10 U.S. to give the Canadian consumer a break." Discuss.

Appendix: Table 8-1

Canadian Balance of Payments: 1965-1970

	1965	1966	1967	1968	1969	1970
			(millions of dollars)			
Current Account						
Receipts						
Exports	8,745	10,326	11,338	13,537	14,874	16,841
Service and Transfer Receipts	2,736	3,070	3,747	3,647	4,221	4,739
Total	11,481	13,396	15,085	17,184	19,095	21,580
Payments						
Imports	8,627	10,102	10,772	12,162	14,014	13,839
Service and Transfer Payments	3,984	4,456	4,812	5,129	5,832	6,444
Total	12,611	14,558	15,584	17,291	19,846	20,283
Current Account Balance	−1,160	−1,162	−1,499	−107	−751	1,297
Capital Account						
Net Long Term Capital Movements	864	1,167	1,347	1,654	2,257	814
Net Short Term Capital Movements	425	−364	−838	−1,198	−1,441	−581
Net Capital Account	1,289	803	519	456	816	233
Change in International Reserves	159	−359	20	349	65	1,663

Source: Bank of Canada, *Statistical Summary.*

Appendix: Table 8-2

Canadian Exchange Rates
(average of noon spot rates)

Year	Value of the Pound Sterling in Canadian Dollars	Value of the United States Dollar in Canadian Dollars
1960	2.723	.970
1961	2.940	1.013
1962	3.002	1.069
1963	3.020	1.079
1964	3.012	1.079
1965	3.014	1.078
1966	3.009	1.077
1967	2.966	1.079
1968	2.579*	1.078
1969	2.574	1.077
1970	2.502	1.044

*Note effect of British Devaluation

Source: Bank of Canada, *Statistical Summary.*

9

Microeconomics and Macroeconomics

How is it that when a firm wishes to expand its operations, it is able to find the workers and the machinery it needs? How do we know that the workers hired by the firm will be able to find housing? That they will be able to spend the wages they receive on goods and services they wish to purchase?

To the student who has already been introduced to microeconomics, these, or ones very similar, will be familiar questions. When they were asked in a microeconomic framework, however, they were answered with the help of a very great simplification: the assumption that individual markets — for labour, for machines, for housing — could each be looked at in isolation, ignoring the effects they might have on other markets and other markets on them.

This assumption allowed us to ask, for example, about the effects of a price change on the demand for a good, "other things being equal" (or *ceteris paribus*); or about the number of workers a firm would hire at a given rate of pay. Our aim was to compare one situation with another after allowing one and only one causal (or *exogenous*) variable to change, tracing through the results of that change as they affected another variable or set of variables. Now that we have taken a look at the macroeconomic approach to economic problems, it is time to take a look at the relationship between micro and macro.

The Concept of Equilibrium

A particularly useful analytic device in trying to answer this type of question is the concept of *equilibrium*. In equilibrium, the state of the system remains the same tomorrow as it is today. Because it is hard to compare systems which are changing (that is, not *in* equilibrium), it is convenient to wait until they "settle" before making comparisons.* That is, we examine a system and compare the positions of equilibrium before and after changing a variable.

From Partial to General Equilibrium

The analytic device of holding all but one of the variables constant and looking at the effects of that single factor in isolation is part of the *partial equilibrium* approach. In a way, it is an attempt by the social scientist to carry out an "experiment" under the same controlled conditions that physical scientists strive for in their work. The difference is that social scientists usually cannot go out and *conduct* this type of experiment. Outside the laboratory, too many things happen at the same time for us to be able to look at the effects of any one of them alone.

Economists occasionally can experiment with the reactions of people to different incomes, or price levels, for example, but there are usually too many other things changing for them to be sure that those were the only important casual variables.

We can get around part of this problem, however, by asking a "What if . . . ?" type of question. "What if" we held all else constant and looked at the quantity of bread (or beer, or automobiles) demanded at different prices for bread (or beer, or automobiles)? "What if" we held all else constant and asked how many workers a firm would employ at different wage rates? These are precisely the types of questions which make up the greatest part of micro-economics.

This does not mean that this is the approach we always want to use, however. A *general theory* looks at all of the relationships between a specified set of variables, a *partial theory* ignores some of the relationships. Thus, our partial equilibrium approach may be useful for some purposes and not for others, where we might require a general approach.

One further fact that should be noted is that a *partial* theory could be more *comprehensive* than a general theory if it included a greater number of variables (although holding their influence constant). An example might help to clear up all of these points. Consider the following general theory:

*There are two basic types of equilibrium, *static* and *dynamic*. In static equilibrium, the variables have constant values in successive periods. In the simplest example of a dynamic equilibrium (there are many different forms), the rates of change in the values are the same in successive periods. Hence, static equilibrium is a special case of this dynamic equilibrium where the rates of change are all zero. This book is concerned primarily with comparisons of static equilibria or *comparative statics*.

1. The demand for beer depends upon the price of beer and the price of gin.
2. The supply of beer is a function of the price of beer and the price of gin.
3. The demand for gin is a function of the price of gin and the price of beer.
4. The supply of gin depends upon the price of gin and the price of beer.
5. The supply of beer must equal the demand for beer.
6. The supply of gin must equal the demand for gin.

This theory could be represented by six equations (we would have to specify the exact relationships, of course) in six unknowns.

$$(1) \quad D_b = D_b(P_b, P_g)$$
$$(2) \quad S_b = S_b(P_b, P_g)$$
$$(3) \quad D_g = D_g(P_g, P_b)$$
$$(4) \quad S_g = S_g(P_g, P_b)$$
$$(5) \quad D_b = S_b$$
$$(6) \quad D_g = S_g$$

(Where D_b is the demand for beer; S_b, the supply of beer; P_b, the price of beer; D_g, the demand for gin; S_g, the supply of gin; P_g, the price of gin).

It is a general theory because it specifies all of the ways in which each variable is expected to affect each other variable. We cannot be certain that there will *be* a general equilibrium solution, or that any equilibrium, if it exists, will be *stable* (that is, will be the point where the system "settles" if it is disturbed and then permitted to come to rest again). Only with more information about the functional relationships in (1) through (4) can we be certain, but assume for the moment that a stable equilibrium solution does exist, and that there is only one such solution.

What type of questions can we answer using this theory? We can ask about the quantities of beer and gin which will be sold, and about their prices, which is the same as finding the equilibrium position for the system. But we can ask much more interesting questions too.

What happens, for example, if tastes change and the demand schedule for gin is shifted up? We can use this theory to look at the effects this has on the price of beer and the amount of beer which will be sold as well as at the direct effects on the price of gin and the quantity of gin sold. It can take into account the possibility that some gin drinkers may switch to beer if the price of gin rises. It can take into account the effect of this substitution on the demands for gin and beer, their prices, and the resulting secondary effects on demand!

In a partial theory, it is these secondary effects which are ignored. The following theory is a partial one, but it is also a more comprehensive one because it allows another variable to enter into the determination of the demand for beer.

1. The demand for beer depends upon the price of beer and the price of gin, *and the temperature.*
2. The supply of beer depends upon the price of beer and the price of gin.
3. The supply of beer must equal the demand for beer.

The number of variables is greater (we have added temperature), so the theory is more comprehensive. But the number of relationships is smaller. This theory provides no way of determining what the price of gin will be (or the temperature, nor how the demand for gin will affect the demand for beer, and so on). It is hence a partial theory, since it does not specify all of the relationships between the five variables.

Expressed in equation form:

$$(1) \quad D_b = D_b(P_b, P_g, T)$$
$$(2) \quad S_b = S_b(P_b, P_g)$$
$$(3) \quad S_b = D_b$$

(Where D_b is the demand for beer; P_b, the price of beer; S_b, the supply of beer; P_g, the price of gin; T, temperature.)

If we want to make predictions about the quantity of beer which will be consumed, we now have two theories to choose from. Which is better? The primary test is empirical: the one which gives the most accurate results. We might want to use one theory for one purpose — for example, the partial theory to make predictions about seasonal beer consumption, where temperature may play an important role — and the other for a different situation like the prediction of total consumption of beer for an entire year.

Which theory is better therefore depends upon the use to which we put it.

Microeconomics, Partial and General Theories

Most of microeconomics deals with partial theories. The behaviour of the individual, the theory of the firm, the

141

behaviour of markets, all are viewed in this way. This is the approach taken for two main reasons. First, we must learn to walk before we can run, and we need practice using simple theories before we turn to more complex ones. Second, we pointed out that the test of any theory's usefulness was, ultimately, its ability to predict. Had we dealt with more comprehensive or more general theories, we might simply have made our task of prediction too difficult to obtain any results at all!

The choice of one type of theory over another is hardly ever a clearcut one. Even at the microeconomic level of analysis, we might want a more complete theory — one which described all of the relationships between a very large number of variables. Obviously, this would be a rather complex task. But it would not be an impossible one. To set out this general theory would be rather cumbersome, but only because of the large number of variables involved, and not because of any serious problems with the mathematics.

Economists have made some progress toward constructing a general model of the economy using a microeconomic approach called *input-output analysis.* *

The most important part of the theory consists of an *input-output table*, a sort of blueprint, or "recipe", which tells us how much of each input is required to produce a specified amount of output, or, if we like, how much output can be produced with given amounts of inputs. This table can be set up to show as detailed a picture of the economy as we wish (although we might have some problems getting all of the data required for a very detailed picture).

The major problem with this approach is that it does not handle changes in the recipes — technological change, for example — very well, because it provides us only with a picture of the system at one moment in time, and with prices given. Because some of the relationships between variables change over time, we have to be careful when we use the theory to make predictions about the real world. Further, because we have to make assumptions about prices and technical conditions, the theory is not really a general one, but merely a first step toward the comprehensive general theory we would like.

For a more detailed discussion of input-output analysis at a relatively simple level, see two articles in Scientific American *by Wassily Leontief, "Input-Output Economics" (1951), and "The Structure of Development" (1963), available as* Scientific American *Offprints 610 and 617 respectively.*

---

*A completely general theory was formulated by the nineteenth century economist Leon Walras; the *Walrasian theory* has so far proven too large to specify, although the system can be described in general mathematical terms. Input-output analysis looks only at a very small part of the Walrasian theory.

Macroeconomics and the Problem of Aggregation

We can see from the above discussion that to build a general equilibrium model of the economy using a micro-economic approach might be a very complicated task indeed. We need some way to simplify the working of the price system; that is the task of macroeconomics. To gain some predictive power, and to reduce a very complex system to one we can handle, we will have to give up some detail. Where microeconomics deals with behaviour of individuals, particular goods, individual firms and factors of production, macroeconomics deals with the aggregates of these units. Thus we deal with *aggregate demand*, *aggregate supply*, "the" *price level*, and "the" *employment level*.

To do this we have to be able to move from the behaviour of individual consumers, for instance, to the behaviour of the aggregate consumption of all individuals, and this generalization can pose some problems. In our partial equilibrium framework, it was probably realistic to assume that the behaviour of one consumer in response to price did not seriously affect the behaviour of other economic units.

As an example, if Jones decides to purchase a new car, we can probably assume away any effects on the price of automobiles due to his increased demand (although his next door neighbour may well decide that he too needs a new car). But if a large number of individuals all decide simultaneously that they want new cars, then they are likely to push up automobile prices. The aggregation of individual demands into aggregate demand hence is not so simple and straightforward as we should like it.

To get around this problem, we make a simplifying assumption that *relative* prices remain stable. In other words, we assume that if one price changes, all others are changed by the same per cent, so that the ratio of any two prices is always the same.* This permits us to neglect changes in individual prices and to look only at "the" price level. To do this, however, we must also assume that the composition of our aggregate of goods and services also remains the same. This permits us to sum the quantity of inputs or outputs in dollar terms, to talk about aggregate supply or demand, and to refer to a single price level for these aggregates.

---

*In the postscript, we will relax this assumption and see what issues are raised for public policy.

At the microeconomic level, economists look at the effects of changes in these relative prices on the demands for individual items. Those relative prices are determined by supply and demand schedules. But we also would like to know how *absolute* prices are established, and that task can only be undertaken via macroeconomics. In this book we have established a framework within which we can begin to examine this and other questions at the aggregate level.

Summary

1.   Partial equilibrium analysis involves the effect of changes in a single variable on the equilibrium position while holding all other things (variables) constant. General equilibrium analysis allows all variables to vary through interaction with each other until the whole system returns to equilibrium.
2.   The comprehensiveness of a theory (partial or general) is a measure of the number of variables or factors considered in the theory.
3.   Microeconomics is most commonly concerned with partial theories. Attempts at more general microeconomic theories (input-output analysis, Walrasian general equilibrium) have limited application because they are too complicated and cumbersome.
4.   Macroeconomics is a form of general theory which attempts to limit the number of variables by aggregating the multitude of prices, supplies, demands, wages and employment levels into single measures of "the" price level, aggregate supply, aggregate demand, "the" employment level, etc.

Questions for Discussion

1.   What does the assumption *ceteris paribus* mean, and how is it important to economists?

2.   Distinguish between partial and general theories, and explain the relationship of comprehensivity to each.

3.   "General theories are better than partial theories, because the partial theories leave out too many variables to be of any use." Discuss.

4.   Explain why "the aggregation problem" worries economists. Why can we not be certain that because individuals consume more as their incomes rise, the level of consumption in the economy will increase as aggregate income rises? (Hint: consider the income *distribution* as well as the income *level* in talking about aggregates.)

5.   Is the Keynesian theory developed here a partial or a general one? Are we holding any variables constant? Are we leaving out any variables which we might want to include in a more comprehensive model? If the model is a partial one, what relationships must we add in order to make it general?

10

Macroeconomic Policy and the Canadian Economy: Some Problems

Unfortunately, the application of theoretical principles to contemporary economic problems in Canada is not nearly as simple as our discussion so far might lead one to believe. In the first place, we have assumed throughout that the economy is in essence one relatively homogeneous unit which acts and reacts to economic stimulae as a unified whole. Secondly, under fiscal policy, we have assumed that the government acts as a single unit. Given the fact that Canada has one federal, ten provincial and innumerable municipal, school, hospital and other regional governments each with powers to spend and often to tax, this assumption becomes highly debatable. Thirdly, Canada is closely aligned with the American economy, not only in terms of markets for Canadian exports and supplies of Canadian imports, but also in terms of the integration of corporate structures, financial markets and even labour markets. The question that arises is to what extent can Canadian policy vary independently of American policy.

In the light of these qualifications, one problem that has received a great deal of attention recently has been the problem of inflation which has developed since the mid-sixties. Since unemployment has occurred at the same time, is the Keynesian analysis relevant or should we look to new theories? To these matters we will devote this chapter.

Regionalism in the Canadian Economy

As we have implied, the Canadian economy is not one homogeneous structure. Rather, it is a combination of six

145

major regions and numerous sub-regions bonded together by a political superstructure. In fact, the prime motive of Confederation over a hundred years ago was to foster an integration of the economies of the various and diverse British North American colonies into a viable political and economic system. As we shall see, Confederation was only partially successful in integrating the regions so as to create a fully complementary national economy.

Canada is usually divided into six major regions: the Atlantic provinces, Quebec, Ontario (the latter two sometimes considered as a single region, Central Canada), the Prairies, British Columbia and the North. The division along provincial boundaries presents some difficulties. For instance, there is a distinct difference between the prairie and the part of the Canadian Shield that passes through some of the prairie provinces. Quebec and Ontario, on the other hand, are in many respects very similar with their industrialization and high population density along the St. Lawrence and natural resource frontier in the northern areas. However, we shall consider them separately, not only because of the obvious political and cultural dichotomy, but because the economic structure and behaviour of the two provinces has been significantly different.

A very brief comparison of the economic structures of the regions may afford a basis for understanding some of the problems for aggregate economic analysis presented by our diverse economy.

The Atlantic provinces have similar development histories, particularly in their reliance on the fisheries, the timber trade, and more recently, pulp and paper, as leading sectors or growth poles. Other primary industries — iron and steel and coal in Nova Scotia, agriculture in Prince Edward Island and parts of New Brunswick — have also been significant in the regional economy. The mark of the Atlantic region has been the reliance on these primary industries, and involvement in Atlantic trade. Recently, as a result of transportation difficulties in relation to central Canada, changes in technology and markets, and relative resource inferiority, these industries have become depressed, leaving the Atlantic region with slow growth and a distressed economy.

Quebec and Ontario had a common early reliance on the fur and timber trades. Since confederation these provinces have become the industrial heartland of Canada. As one authority has written, "exports from both Quebec and Ontario came to supply the rest of Canada rather than customers abroad. Together the two provinces constitute the industrial heart of Canada, and pulp and paper and

While these regions are the most commonly discussed, there are, of course, regional differences even within provinces. The Gaspé, the Niagara Peninsula, the Manitoba Interlake, the Okanogan Valley and similar areas each have their own specific setting, problems and relationships within the provincial, regional, national and international economies.

146

hydroelectric power loom large in both economies. Both provinces, too, have experienced mineral booms since the end of the war".* Both remain highly dependent on primary resource production.

Nevertheless, important differences must be noted. Heavy industry is concentrated in Ontario, light industries in Quebec. Also, Quebec has a larger marginal primary industry group, particularly small mixed farming.

The prairie region is, of course, noted for the primacy of its agricultural industry, in particular wheat and other grains, and to a lesser extent cattle. The extractive mineral industries, however, have begun to play a greater role — oil in Alberta, nickel in Manitoba and potash in Saskatchewan being the most notable. Manitoba has a somewhat more diversified economy, producing some manufacturing output for the region. Nevertheless, as a result of both policy and natural and acquired advantages, the bulk of the region's manufactured goods are imported from outside the region, concentrating in central Canada.

British Columbia has traditionally been somewhat isolated from the rest of the Canadian economy by the transportation barrier posed by the Rocky Mountains. Its development has been very different from that of the other western provinces, having very limited commercial agriculture. Nevertheless, its development has occurred with the exploitation of natural resources of fish, lumber and minerals in earlier decades, supplemented by hydro power and pulp and paper in the post-war period.

The *northern area* of Canada is largely underdeveloped, with a limited population in traditional semi-subsistence pursuits supplemented by nascent mineral exploitation and limited defense settlements. For our purposes of discussing stabilization policy we will not be too concerned with the northern region.

Before proceeding further, we should note the over-all trading pattern of the Canadian economy, a pattern fostered by the national policy in the formative years of the Canadian nation and one which has persisted for a century. The western regions and the Atlantic provinces are primarily natural resource areas producing primary products for export or for the manufacturing region in central Canada. The same can be said for the northern parts of Ontario and Quebec. The export markets, however, are not the same for the different regions. American markets are

*R. E. Caves and R. H. Holton, *The Canadian Economy*, Cambridge: Harvard University Press, 1961, p. 146.

most important to B.C. and the Atlantic regions, although B.C. has increasingly sold to the Japanese market. Outside of mineral exports, prairie export markets are centred in Europe and the Far East. The resource industries of central Canada feed the Great Lakes industrial complex in both the U.S. and Canada.

Let us now show, in a descriptive way, some of the implication of this structure for Canadian policy. As is now familiar, $AD = C + I + G + (X - M)$. Let us assume that we begin from a position of full employment without inflation across Canada. Then, as a consequence of a bumper crop in Russia, Canada's (the prairies') wheat exports fall. As a result there will be a decline in aggregate demand. Consumption will of course also fall, affecting all regions which supply the prairie consumer. But this will have a much smaller affect in other regions than in the prairies. The result will probably be deficient demand, producing unemployment in the prairies with only marginal effects on the rest of the Canadian economy. What could the government do about it? Let us assume that the federal government decreases taxes. This would increase consumption in all parts of Canada. Only a fraction of this would apply to the prairie economy. A likely result would be an increase in the demand for manufactured goods produced in central Canada. This would probably produce demand inflation in Ontario without solving the prairie unemployment problem. In the long run, of course, we might expect unemployed workers to move from the prairie region to central Canada — but this is a very long-term expectation.

A specific example of this kind of problem is the Atlantic region. The decline in the demand for fish exports, for Nova Scotia coal and iron ore, and for shipbuilding and related maritime services brought on by construction of the St. Lawrence Seaway, has produced depressed demand for the output of the region. As a result, aggregate demand has in recent years never reached the full employment point. Using fiscal or monetary policy at the national level would almost inevitably produce inflationary demand in central Canada before the spill-over of aggregate demand to the Atlantic provinces brought full employment there. In the long run, as we have suggested in our prairie example, labour would leave the Atlantic provinces, tending to reduce aggregate supply and thus ultimately to produce full employment. Labour *has* been leaving the Atlantic provinces but this has the additional affect of reducing their consumption demand also. The fall in aggregate *supply* through a decline in the labour force has not been sufficient to offset the decline in *demand*,

and the result has been a depressed regional economy even when, over-all, the Canadian economy has been producing close to full capacity.

These two examples should suffice to show what kind of problems Canada faces. Resources do not necessarily move between regions freely enough so that the blunt instruments of macro policy can bring aggregate supply and demand to equilibrium at full employment without inflation in all regions of the economy. This is particularly true since autonomous changes in aggregate demand affect different regions quite selectively. In large measure this is because a major source of instability in aggregate demand is beyond regional or national control, originating in foreign demand which is not sensitive to stabilization policy in Canada.

We may now introduce a second problem with our theoretical application of fiscal and monetary policy in Canada. We should point out that monetary policy cannot discriminate between provinces and regions. On the other hand, it is possible to restrict spending in some regions relative to others or possibly even to implement different tax rates regionally. However, the political constraints suggest that the scope for this is limited.

Compounding this problem are the fiscal powers of the provincial and municipal governments. There is no guarantee that the provincial and municipal governments will introduce policies complementary to those of the federal government. At the same time, the two junior levels of government spend almost 60 per cent of total government spending. For the municipal governments it is virtually impossible to co-ordinate or plan over-all fiscal policy because of the sheer numbers of jurisdictions and the fact that local taxation and spending is closely related to specific service needs in the local communities.

Regional problems would arise even if there were no regional governments, of course, but the problems of co-ordinating national development are made all the more difficult by the competing aims and claims of the various authorities.

It is at the provincial level that co-ordination might appear more feasible. However, here too there are serious difficulties. Let us take the example of Quebec, which has in recent years suffered relatively high unemployment. Theory might suggest a deficit finance policy at the provincial level. However, the more limited ability of the province to borrow compared with the federal government, the leakage of the multiplier effects to other regions, and the possible conflict with federal monetary policy, severely constrain provincial action. To some extent the policy of tax equilization payments by the federal government (which transfers some tax revenues from the richer to the poorer provinces, permitting a higher spending level in the poorer regions at lower tax levels than

149

would otherwise be the case) improves the potential for regional stabilization policies, but the regional disparities are too great to be significantly offset.

At the same time that Quebec may be suffering unemployment equilibrium, a province like British Columbia may be approaching an inflationary demand situation. There the political costs of reduced government spending and higher taxes at the provincial level may override national stabilization goals, particularly since responsibility for inflation can usually be laid to the federal government.

Provincial stabilization goals may also conflict with economic growth criteria, given the competition between provincial governments for new industry. In our example, while national policy might call for high taxes in British Columbia to restrict investment spending and consumption — shifting investment to Quebec — such an altruistic policy does not conform to the political reality.

These illustrations should give some idea of the problems of an integrated monetary and fiscal policy in the Canadian economy with its regional economic structure and fragmented government structure. These problems do not eliminate the need or the desirability for intelligent stabilization policies — they merely limit the effectiveness of such policies in a non-centralized state.

Canada and United States - Unequal Partners

Another type of problem facing Canadian policy makers in the area of macro stabilization policy is the strong influence of the United States' economy. As we have pointed out previously, over a quarter of Canada's aggregate demand originates abroad. This means that Canada has little or no control over this segment of demand. The largest single customer for Canadian exports is the United States. Thus, the state of demand for Canadian goods in the American economy is one of the most important single influences on the state of the Canadian economy, and an influence over which Canada has little, if any, control.

Secondly, as we have shown with fiscal policy, changes in taxes may be needed to decrease or increase demand depending on the state of the economy. However, it is generally conceded that because of the integration of Canada-U.S. corporate structures, a common capital market and relatively free labour mobility between the two countries, the tax policy in Canada cannot differ greatly from that in the U.S. For instance, a rise in Canadian corporation taxes may encourage Canadian subsidiaries to transfer internal prices so that profits accrue in the United States. The effect on aggregate demand, therefore, may be much less than anticipated.

The common North American capital market has a tendency to limit the effectiveness of monetary policy carried on independently in Canada. For instance, if Canada instituted a tight monetary policy to moderate investment demand, the effect of a rise in interest rates would attract an inflow from the United States particularly in the large corporations who have direct access to funds on the American market. Again, the effectiveness of Canadian policy may very well be much less than desired.

This is by no means an exhaustive analysis of the problem in implementing macro policy. It is merely indicative of the nature of the difficulties in translating aggregate economic theory into realistic and effective policy. As a further illustration, we will now look in more detail at the problem of inflation that has occurred in Canada in the latter years of the 1960s.

Inflation and Canadian Policy

We are by now reasonably familiar with the concept of demand inflation — excess aggregate demand at full employment producing a rise in the price level. Symptoms of demand-pull inflation, therefore, are a low level of unemployment and rising prices. In the real world, we should not expect unemployment to be zero. The reasons for this are frictional, seasonal and structural unemployment. By "frictional" we mean that some people are always changing jobs in response to normal market pressures and personal choice, school graduates are entering the labour force, and so on. Even though there are jobs available for these people, it may take a few days or weeks for supply and demand to match up. Thus, there is unemployment due to "friction" in the labour market which is normal and unavoidable. Secondly, there are, particularly in Canada, jobs which are sensitive to seasonal influences — due to weather (e.g. construction), natural resource cycles (e.g. fishing), holiday demands (e.g. tourist industries), or similar types of influence. Given the structure of the Canadian economy, it is difficult to conceive of eliminating entirely this seasonal kind of unemployment, although policy can be directed at promoting industries with complementary seasonal peaks.

Germany in the early 1920s provides us with an example of runaway inflation leading to an eventual collapse of the value of the German currency. When the government tried to finance the rebuilding of the economy after the war by issuing new currency (selling bonds to the central bank), the main result was an increase in the price level. From the end of 1919 to the end of 1923, prices rose eighteen trillion per cent (18,000,000,000,000%)!

151

Thirdly, people's tastes are constantly shifting — for example from cotton wear to artificial fibres, or from food products to services. The shift in particular demand takes place before supply shifts. Thus, we say that the structure of demand has changed while the structure of supply has not yet adjusted. In the adjustment process people will become unemployed in the declining demand sector. In time labour will shift to the rising demand sector, but until this process takes place, "structural" unemployment will result. Because of these factors, Canadian policy-makers have come to regard three per cent unemployment as "full employment".

At the same time we would not expect perfect price stability at or even just below full employment. Prices and wages tend to be inflexible downwards and, as the structure of demand shifts, the initial result will be a rise in prices for the more popular goods and services, but the prices of the goods and services from the declining industries will usually not fall significantly. As a result, *average* prices will tend to rise slowly. Secondly (although it has proven difficult to assess its importance), it has been argued that improvements are introduced in goods and services from one year to the next. Therefore, small rises in price may reflect nothing more than an improvement in quality and are therefore not real price increases. Thirdly, wages tend to rise in response to productivity increases in the growing industries. In other industries where productivity is growing more slowly, wages nevertheless tend to rise at a similar pace. This necessitates a price increase in these low productivity growth industries and a slow rise in the average price level. For these reasons, policy-makers aim at "reasonable price stability" which permits a rate of price increase of around two per cent per year.

Therefore, we would tend to identify demand-pull inflation when unemployment falls to around 3 per cent or less with prices rising at more than 2 per cent per year. Let us now look at the Canadian price and unemployment record in the 1960s.

Chile during the 1960s experienced rapid but not runaway inflation, and real growth of the economy continued at nearly 5% per year even though prices rose by as much as 50% per year. Chileans seemed to accept the inflation as part of the economy, and while the country faced problems common to all of the less developed areas of the world, inflation did not seem to have made those difficulties any more serious.

TABLE 10-1

Year	% Unemployment	% Change in Consumer Price Index
1960	7.0	1.2
1961	7.1	0.9
1962	5.9	1.2
1963	5.5	1.8
1964	4.7	1.7
1965	3.9	2.5
1966	3.6	3.7
1967	4.1	3.6
1968	4.8	4.1
1969	4.7	4.5
1970	5.9	3.3

It is obvious from the above table that, since 1965, the Canadian economy has had both price inflation and excess unemployment. Does this mean that our theoretical analysis is incorrect. Obviously it does indicate that our simple model in inadequate.

The first alternative explanation to Keynesian demand-pull inflation is the concept of "cost-push" inflation — that price rises are not due to excess demand but to rising costs that are not responsive to market conditions and which firms are able to pass on in consumer or producer prices. Specific variations of cost-push inflation could be characterized by "wage-push", "profit-push", "interest-push", or "import-price-push". We can explain them in this manner. Wage-push might exist where unionized workers are able to use their bargaining strength to increase wages. To cover their increased wage costs, firms increase prices even though unemployment may exist. Profit-push operations occur in a similar way. Firms try to increase profits purely by raising prices. Normally this is only possible where there is little or no competition in the market, but, for most major Canadian industries, it is not unrealistic to claim that this is the case. A third varient, although not much discussed, is related to interest rates as a cost. A rise in interest rates raises firms' costs and prices in the same manner as wages or profits. The trouble is that, while high interest rates (tight monetary policy) are implemented to control demand-pull inflation, they may also contribute to potential cost-push inflation! It has even been argued by some that rising interest rates have been a major component of recent increases in consumer prices in Canada, due primarily via the micro effects of interest rates on housing costs.

A rise in import prices can affect consumer prices both directly and indirectly. Let us assume for instance that the United States is experiencing inflation. The first effect follows readily — the prices of imported United States-produced final products sold in Canada rise and, since they are part of our consumers' basket of goods, our price index rises. This effect through consumer prices is not the only, or possibly even, the most important, effect. Canada imports a very high proportion of its machinery and equipment for producing goods and services, as well as a large number of components for assembly into final products. Increases in the prices of these goods in the U.S., therefore, raise the costs of *Canadian*-produced goods, and these increases are passed on to the Canadian consumer. Indeed, the importance of imported inflation may be greater than is usually considered. The Economic Council of Canada in its 1969 review points to this conclusion.

> In Canada, it is difficult to maintain that current inflation is a reflection of excessive demand pressures, for the Canadian economy has been operating with at least a moderate over-all margin of slack since 1967. On the other hand, in the United States the problem of price and cost inflation has been very much one of excessive demand, aggravated by the impact on the economy of the war in Vietnam. Until some easing of price and cost increases takes place in the United States, Canadian policies to deal with domestic price and cost problems will be handicapped. Further, fiscal and monetary restraint could conceivably result simply in higher rates of unemployment and slack with no more than marginal effects on current rates of increase in prices and costs. Moreover, tighter restraint in Canada this year is likely to have its main impact on the economy next year. And if excess demand pressures in the United States are brought under control by the latter part of 1969, the principle result of stringent demand policy restraints in Canada this year might well be seriously mistimed to push the economy into poor economic performance*.

It should be noted that restrictive monetary and fiscal policy can have little effect on imported inflation. Therefore, it has been argued that, until the United States brings its inflation under control (which has been ascribed to excess demand due to expenditures on the Vietnam war, and the decision to finance the war from borrowings rather than from increased taxation), Canada can do little to control its price level without sending unemployment to unacceptable heights.

Inflation in Canada may also be partly ascribed to a form of structural inflation. In part this is a variation of Keynesian demand-pull inflation. First, consider the following table. Note that, although average unemployment in Canada as a whole never approached what we have defined as full employment, it did so in Ontario.** Since

TABLE 10-2

Unemployment by Region

Year	Canada	B.C.	Prairies	Ontario	Quebec	Atlantic
1964	4.7	5.3	3.2	3.2	6.4	7.8
1965	3.9	4.1	2.6	2.5	5.4	7.4
1966	3.6	4.5	2.1	2.5	4.7	6.4
1967	4.1	5.1	2.4	3.1	5.3	6.6
1968	4.8	5.9	2.9	3.5	6.5	7.3
1969	4.7	5.0	2.9	3.1	6.9	7.6
1970	5.9	7.7	4.4	4.3	7.9	7.6

*Sixth Annual Review, Economic Council of Canada, p. 163.

**It was even lower in the Prairie provinces, but for different reasons. As we suggested earlier, the Prairie economy depends heavily on demand for its primary products abroad, which was quite strong during this period. Also, it is more difficult to measure unemployment in agricultural production activities, so the figures may underestimate "underemployment" by neglecting people who have jobs but are not employed in their most efficient occupations.

154

Ontario is the main supplier of manufactured goods to the rest of Canada, demand pressure in Ontario may be translated directly into rising consumer prices and indirectly into cost-push inflation in other regions. Fiscal and monetary policies designed to reduce the level of demand in Ontario have a deflationary effect on *all* parts of the country and may have contributed to producing serious regional unemployment.

Second, consider Table 10-3. Note that the contribution of different industrial sectors to price increases has been markedly different. Several interpretations are possible. Nevertheless the pattern is consistent with the explanation that the trend to urbanization and the rise in incomes have resulted in shifts in demand which were not matched by supply shifts or a growth in productivity. The greater the rate of structural shift in demand, the more rapid the resultant price increases would be. The sixties can be considered a decade of relatively rapid change in the structure of demand. Restrictive fiscal and monetary policy may have slowed down the shift in demand but it may also, as in the case of housing, have slowed the shift in supply.

If you think we've really sidestepped the question of who is to blame for inflation, you're largely correct. Economists have done a much better job on the diagnosis cure of unemployment (although even in that area, their models are far from perfect), than they have on inlfation. The discussion here should serve to show just how complicated the problem is, particularly in Canada.

TABLE 10-3

Contribution to Inflation by Sector

	1st Quarter 1961 – 1st Quarter 1966	1st Quarter 1966 – 1st Quarter 1969
Percentage change in Consumer Price Index	10.0	14.4
Proportion of change due to price change in:		
Durable manufactures	−5	5
Non-durable manufactures (excluding food)	20	25
Food	40	20
Services (excluding shelter)	25	20
Shelter	20	30
Total	100	100

Source: Economic Council of Canada *Sixth Annual Review*, 1969, p. 149.

Thus, from this "case study" of Canadian problems, we can see the difficulty in analyzing a real-world situation in terms of our simple model. Nevertheless, without our model we could not have proceeded this far. It should remind us that we cannot ignore the particular structural and regional characteristics of our economy, the influence of our large international sector and our integration into the American economy, and the effect on price adjustments in the micro markets as a result of changes in the structure of demand and in macro policy.

Stop - Go! - The Economics of Lags

In the late sixties, the Canadian government gave priority in economic policy to the curbing of inflation. This was attempted with the kind of fiscal and monetary policies we would have recommended from orthodox Keynesian theory. Taxes were increased, government expenditures curtailed, the money supply tightened and interest rates raised dramatically. All of the economic signal lights said "Stop!".

Prices ceased rising significantly (at least temporarily) late in 1970 but the spring of 1971 also saw unemployment rise to its highest level, 6.7% (seasonally adjusted, April) in a decade. Government expenditure began to increase slowly, the money supply loosened and interest rates began falling — the economic signals switched to "Go!".

The swings between unacceptable inflation and unacceptable unemployment have sometimes lead to public criticism of economic theories and of "the experts" (i.e., economists). Surely the whole point of Keynesian economics is that these swings between inflation and unemployment can be ironed out through judicious manipulation of fiscal and monetary policies. We have already pointed out some of the problems that occur, however, because of the division of taxing and spending power among several levels of government and because of fluctuations in export demand. Nevertheless, there is another major problem that affects all countries which attempt to use stabilization policies to moderate economic swings. This is the problem of *lags*.

Lags simply refer to the fact that changing the injections into or drains out of the income flow takes some time to have its full effect on the economy. (Note that we assumed away this problem in the theory by making our adjustment process virtually instantaneous.) Like an old fashioned water pump where it is necessary to pump for some time before water is drawn up to the spout, a change in government policy must precede by some time the desired change in aggregate demand. Thus, the implementation of a new policy must *lead* changes in economic conditions so that their effect is felt as economic conditions actually alter, not after. Let us take an example approximating recent experience.

In conditions of rising prices the government has taken a restrictive fiscal and monetary policy. As these policies in Canada (and in the United States) begin to affect output, prices will moderate and unemployment will begin to rise If the authorities have not anticipated this rise in unemployment, they will have to begin to reverse policies *after unemployment has already begun to increase.* It is unlikely (short of the government going out and hiring all of the unemployed itself) that new economic policies will have an immediate effect.

For example, a cut in taxes, even if it could be arranged on short notice, will have its effects over the whole year, in "twelve easy installments". A rise in government expenditure on construction usually takes months to plan before the full effect is felt. Businessmen, seeing interest rates falling are likely to "wait and see", because their investment decisions are based on expectations of future demand. With unemployment rising, this has a depressing influence on business expectations and thus on investment even with interest rates falling and money becoming more readily available. It has been said that you can pull on a string (restrict investment by tight money), but you can't *push* on it (create investment by easy money if expectations are depressed).

Good economic forecasting can allow a government to lead with the appropriate policies so that the swings are modified before they catch momentum through changed expectations. A second partial solution is to reduce the lag time. Some countries (Sweden probably has the lead here) have attempted this through such measures as producing detailed construction plans for publicly financed buildings which can be activated on very short notice, and controlling more strictly the rate of investment flow through special funds. Implimentation of these measures is in the hands of permanent economic agencies rather than requiring legislative action, and constitute a form of short-term economic planning.

A third partial solution is the expansion of automatic stabilizers. One such suggestion for the Canadian economy is to have the level and duration of unemployment insurance benefits vary with the rate of unemployment. (This could also be done regionally.) As unemployment began to rise, so would unemployment benefits, thus injecting more consumption demand into the economy. (Remember that unemployment insurance benefits are transfer payments; raising their level gives the same effect

Things are not quite hopeless, however. If the bank rate really does serve to let investors know what future government policy will be, and investors react accordingly, then expectations about the rate of interest can play an important role in generating investment.

157

on consumption as lowering taxes.) On the basis of recent experience, Canada's record in dealing with lags does not appear to have been impressive. This is one reason why alternatives to monetary and fiscal policies to control inflation have been gaining adherents recently.

Incomes Policy - An Alternative?

The use of Keynesian monetary and fiscal tools to control inflation and unemployment in Canada, as we have seen, is not as simple or straightforward as our theory might have suggested. Not only is there the problem of lags, but even if all lags were correctly forecast and sufficient lead time utilized, we still have not solved the problems of regional imbalances and structural shifts (long term problems), nor can we isolate Canada — under existing economic relationships — from American fluctuations or from cost-push pressures originating outside Canada.* These factors have led to the acceptance of the idea of a trade-off between unemployment and inflation. Advocates of this view argue that we have a choice represented in the following diagram (known as the Phillips curve after the British economist who first wrote about it).

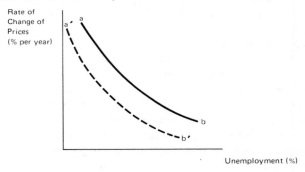

FIGURE 10-1

Any policies which would reduce the residual structural or seasonal unemployment, regional or cost-push inflation influences, would shift the trade-off curve towards the origin (downwards to the left — i.e., to a'b'). Many policies have been devised such as manpower policies, the retraining and movement of unemployed labour to reduce seasonal and structural unemployment, and anti-combines policies to reduce the ability of firms to fix or raise prices

*Cost-push inflation could presumably be controlled by restricting AD. For example, if imported machinery rises in price, tending to raise the prices of goods produced by such machinery, the authorities could presumably prevent the average price level from rising significantly by depressing aggregate buying power. However, the result would almost invariably be a jump in unemployment.

even under conditions of less than full employment. However, emphasis has been directed increasingly to incomes policies as an alternative to more orthodox measures.

What is an "incomes policy"? It has been defined as government measures to promote "the kind of evolution of incomes which is consistent with their economic objectives, and in particular with price stability".* The argument is as follows. If government uses fiscal and monetary policy to produce full employment, some inflation will result even before all of the unemployment is mopped up. To control such inflationary pressures, controls, either legislative or moral, need be utilized to restrict prices, wages, profits or rents from contributing to the cost push. (What about interest payments? A tricky question, as discussed earlier.) In theory, the ideal incomes policy would hold the increase in all forms of income to the proportional increase in the real output of the economy from year to year. Unfortunately, as the critics rightly point out, this assumes that the existing distribution of incomes is justified or desirable. Even if this were true (and that is doubtful), who could prove it?

This is another area where economists are forced either to take the value judgements of others, or to make their own. Economic theory, which is just the organization of logical relationships, can take us only so far. It cannot say whether something is "good" or "bad" unless criteria are given for making that judgement.

Incomes policies, such as the U.S. guidelines in the mid-sixties, the British prices and incomes policies during the Labour government and the moral strictures of Canada's Prices and Incomes Commission in recent years, are not primarily macroeconomic measures. Rather they are microeconomic — trying to hold prices and factor payments relatively constant in all markets in order that aggregate demand can achieve a full employment level without excess demand or market power producing price increases in specific sectors.

Incomes policies have, however, definite limits. They cannot control unemployment, and only in the very short run can they supress demand inflation. Even under ideal conditions, an incomes policy must appear "fair" or it will become ineffective through evasion or outright opposition. At best, therefore, it is not a substitute for macro policy but rather a supplement to allow such policy full effective range by minimizing or controlling the effects of market inflexibilities and imperfections. At the same time, if an incomes policy works to retard adjustments to market pressures by artificially holding down prices, wages and other factor payments, then the micro results can produce a lowering of the aggregate output of the economy and thus, in the long run, feed potential inflation. This is another illustration of the problems of integrating macro and micro

*See D. C. Smith, *Incomes Policies*, Economic Council of Canada, Special Study No. 4, 1966, p. 5.

and short run and long run economic policies.

Summary

1.   Difficulties in applying the Keynesian model to the Canadian economy occur because of the regional nature of the economy, the practical impossibility of a single fiscal policy covering all of the multi-levels of government, and the integration of the Canadian with the American economy.

2.   In the real world, "full employment without inflation" is considered to have been achieved if less than three per cent are unemployed and the price level is rising at less than two per cent per year. Keynesian theory would suggest that unemployment greater than 3 per cent should not occur without prices stabilizing, or price increases over 2 per cent per annum should not occur without full employment.

3.   Cost-push inflation and structural inflation are two alternative theories to Keynesian demand-pull inflation to explain the coincidence of high rates of price increase with moderate unemployment.

Postscript

In Chapter 9 we showed how the economist, by aggregating prices in each market for goods and services into one price level, and aggregating supply and demand in each market into single aggregate supply and demand schedules, could simplify the working of the economy into a manageable and useful macro model. In doing so, however, we had to sacrifice something. What we have sacrificed is a knowledge of what is happening in any one of the individual markets. We can see that, if aggregate demand is decreased by fiscal or monetary policy, this should dampen any tendency for prices to rise *in aggregate*. This same policy, however, may in fact cause *some* specific prices to increase. It may also have distributional effects by reallocating real and money incomes among social groups. What do we mean by this? Let us take a few specific examples.

For some reason, this often comes out as "physical policy" on the examination books of students. We know you won't make that mistake.

Interest Rate as a Price

We have considered the interest rate as a major determinant of aggregate demand through its effect on investment and thus aggregate demand. It is, therefore, an instrument which government can use to stabilize the economy. But interest is also a *price* — for our purposes the price of credit, or money. What happens when monetary policy is tightened, raising interest rates? First, all those people who have ownership of money have their incomes raised relative to others in the economy. (They receive higher interest payments.) Second, costs are raised in some markets such as the housing market where credit restriction and higher

161

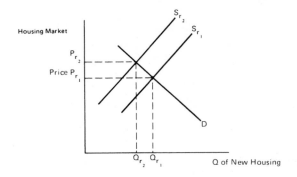

FIGURE P-1

mortgage rates tend to decrease the supply of new housing. In Figure P-1 we can see the example where the interest rate (a cost of providing homes) shifts the supply curve upwards, raising the cost and reducing the supply of housing. To some extent, demand will also be reduced (since people have less income to spend than before), but it is unlikely to be significant relative to the supply effect. These people just entering the housing market at this time, therefore, will have suffered a fall in real income.

Fiscal Policy

As a second example we might look at some micro and distributive effects of government expenditures. For illustrative purposes we shall consider the education industry. In a period of inflationary pressures, the government would want to restrain aggregate demand by reducing government expenditure. But, if the cut in expenditure takes the form of a decline in money for education and training, the micro effects could be both considerable and long-lasting. Let us assume that, as a result of such a cutback, the supply of new engineers to the market is slowed down temporarily. This is illustrated in the following Figure P-2. The effect of the macro policy, therefore, is to change the potential supply of engineers, raising wages over what they would have been without a change in educational expenditure as part of fiscal policy.*

Changes in taxes or transfer payments also have micro effects. Remember that all indirect taxes (sales taxes, excise taxes, customs, duties, business taxes, etc.) are costs

*In the short-run demand may also be shifted downward as a result of a decline in equilibrium income, but such an effect would likely be small compared to the shift in supply.

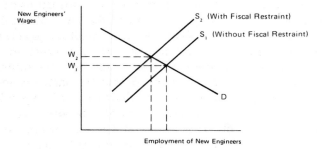

New Engineers' Wages

S_2 (With Fiscal Restraint)

S_1 (Without Fiscal Restraint)

W_2

W_1

D

Employment of New Engineers

FIGURE P-2

of production that enter into the determination of the supply curve in any given market. The kind of tax change can also have important distributive effects. Let us say that, to control inflationary pressure, the government increases taxes on beer. This will raise the cost of beer in the micro market, raising its price and redistributing real income proportionately away from beer-drinkers. The distributional effects of a similar dampening effect on aggregate demand through increased income taxes (or through a cut in transfer payments) would perhaps be very different.

Distribution of Private and Public Goods

In general, therefore, we can see that macro policy is not neutral in its effects. This has given rise to a concern by a number of economists about the relative quantitites of *private* and *public* goods. Since the Second World War, most western countries have faced more years of inflationary pressures than they have of deficient demand. This has meant that stabilization policy has been marked more often by fiscal and monetary restraint than by expansion. But every time fiscal policy is restrictive, it means a restriction in expenditure on public goods relative to private goods. Thus J. K. Galbraith has argued we have produced "private affluence and public squalor". Similarly, the years of restraint have tended to restrict housing expansion both by the effect of tight monetary policy on the private housing market and of tight fiscal policy on the public housing market (since the latter is considered an easy "tap" to turn off and on in fiscal policy). We have now got the apparent paradox that housing shortages in many western countries are blamed on too much prosperity!

For more on public versus private goods, see any introductory text on public finance.

163

We have now (we hope) brought the reader full circle — from a consideration of how the individual markets in our economy are aggregated into measures of total economic activity, what determines the level of total activity and how this level can be influenced by government policy for purposes of stabilization; and how, in turn, these stabilization policies react back on the individual markets. Far too often it appears that this last connection, between macro policy and the allocation of expenditure between sectors, of income between factors and social groups, and the determination of specific prices, specific supply and demand schedules, is ignored. Again we can have the apparent paradox that policies to control inflation can raise costs and prices in specific markets. It is to be hoped that the examples given clarify this problem and close the conceptual circle.

Summary

1.   Interest rates are both a macro regulator and a micro price. Monetary policy to raise interest rates to control inflation may at the same time raise prices of goods and services which embody significant interest costs.
2.   Fiscal policy may have both micro and distributive effects which affect the prices of specific goods and services and the allocation of income among sectors in the economy.

Questions for Discussion

1.   Discuss the merits and demerits of having districts of the Bank of Canada so that monetary policy can be tailored to the needs of individual regions.

2.   René Lévesque has suggested that a separate Quebec could have a common currency with the rest of Canada. Do you agree? Why or why not?

3.   "Cost push inflation is a myth! Pushing up costs doesn't change aggregate demand and if aggregate demand doesn't change, how can inflation occur?" Discuss.

4.   If, because of the nature of Canada's economy, you had to choose between 4% inflation with 2% unemployment or 2% inflation with 4% unemployment, which would you choose? What are the costs of these alternatives?

5.   "There is no such thing as a non-discriminatory fiscal and monetary policy. No matter what you do, you help or hurt some people or groups more than others either through specific price changes, income changes or the like." Discuss.

6.   List the possible benefits and costs of an incomes policy (price, wage, rent and profits control). To what extent would such a policy be possible in Canada?

Some Tools of the Economist —
Appendix on the Use of Graphs and
Mathematical Expressions

The student exposed for the first time to formal economics may feel intimidated by our use of graphs and other mathematical expressions. However, as students get the hang of it they will find that the old adage still holds — "a picture is worth a thousand words". After all, a graph is just a "picture" of something which otherwise would have to be described in words, with much less precision, or in tables of figures which are difficult to grasp. Mathematical equations and expressions are merely shorthand ways of expressing the economic behaviour pictured in our graphs.

Take the following example. You are asked the question, how much sales tax is Mr. Machinist going to pay in any given year? Obviously, even if you know that the rate of sales tax is 5%, you can't answer the question until you know how much he spends. If he spends $100, then Mr. Machinist pays $5 in sales tax; but if he spends $5,000, his tax bill is $250. This same relationship can be shown in tabular form.

Mr. Machinist's Purchases (per year)	Mr. Machinist's Sales Tax Bill (per year)
$50	$2.50
$200	$10.00
$500	$25.00
$1000	$50.00
$5000	$250.00

Such a table indicates that there is a systematic relationship between purchases and sales tax paid. For the economist, this sort of relationship can usually be presented much more clearly as a graph. In the following diagram the horizontal (or X) axis represents the independent vari-

Because the amount of sales tax paid depends upon the level of spending, we call the tax the dependent variable. Spending is therefore the independent variable.

165

able — the purchases our machinist makes. On the vertical (or Y) axis, we record the values of the dependent variable, sales taxes, the level of which depends upon the purchases of our consumer. As you can see, for each level of expenditure by Mr. Machinist, we can determine immediately the tax paid directly from the graph. For example, purchases of $4,000 would entail tax payments of $200 as indicated at points a and b. Thus, Figure A-1 illustrates the behavioural relationship between two economic variables.

People occasionally graph two unrelated variables — check to make sure the diagrams you see used don't make this mistake.

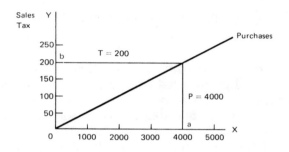

FIGURE A-1

It is only one step further to express this same relationship between sales tax and expenditures in pure mathematical form. We know that everytime Mr. Machinist spends one dollar, he must pay 5% of one dollar in sales tax. Therefore, we can always calculate his sales tax by taking 5% of his purchases, It is obvious, therefore, that $T = s \times P$, where T = sales tax; s = rate of sales tax; and P = value of purchases.

This is just a special case of the straight line relationship between two economic variables. The more general case could be illustrated by our machinist who pays not only a sales tax but also a poll tax (a fixed tax levied once a year) of $50. How do we then determine the total tax bill of Mr. Machinist? Well, regardless of whether he spends anything or not, he still must pay his poll tax. Therefore, his total taxes would be his poll tax ($50), plus his sales tax (which remains as a function of his purchases); or, $T = T_0 + s \times P$ where T_0 is the poll tax, or the total tax *when purchases are 0*. Graphically, this can be shown as follows in Figure A-2, with the poll tax being what is called the *Y intercept* (that is, the value on the Y axis when the value on the X axis is 0).

166

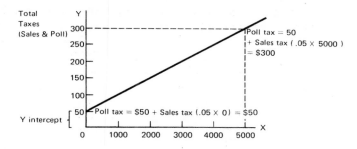

FIGURE A-2

As you can see, our first case shown in Figure A-1 is just a special case of the above where the Y intercept (the tax bill when purchases are 0) is zero. For any straight line relationship between two variables, the above equation holds — Y (the value of the dependent variable) = Y_0 (the value of Y when the independent variable, or X, is 0) + m (the rate at which Y increases with every increase in X, called the *slope*) times X (the value of the independent variable). The corresponding graphical values are shown below ($Y = Y_0 + mX$).

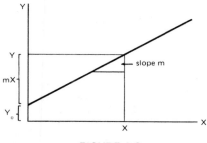

FIGURE A-3

So far we have only illustrated one particular type of relationship — a straight line behavioural relationship between two variables. Curved relationships are more difficult to handle mathematically, but they remain easy to read on a graph. Unless we have a good reason for believing that the relationship between two variables is best represented by a curve, we stick to straight lines!

We can work with three or more variables easily enough by using equations but we'd rather not have to draw them.

167

Actually, we are not being very precise when we call time the independent variable, because time does not cause the tax change.

A very common type of relationship that we see in books and newspapers almost daily is the *time series*. In this case, the independent variable is time. Using our original example, we could illustrate the pattern of Mr. Machinist's purchases over a number of years. In tabular form they might look like this.

Year	Purchases
1961	2,000
1962	2,400
1963	2,400
1964	2,300
1965	2,600
1966	2,800
1967	2,600
1968	3,100
1969	3,200
1970	3,400

When we plot the behaviour of Mr. Machinist's purchases over a number of years, we can conclude that there is an overall tendency for purchases to rise with time, subject to some fluctuations. This can be seen quite clearly in the graphical picture (Figure A-4). We can summarize by saying that the *trend* in purchases is upward, but in any given year purchases may vary from this trend. Usually, the economist goes to statistics to find what is the trend. We can then say that purchases are a function of time. Mathematically, $P = f(t)$, which is just a shorthand way of saying that his purchases are a function of time without saying exactly what the relationship *is*.

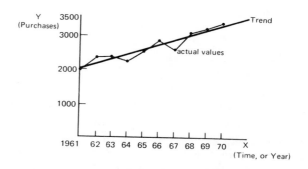

FIGURE A-4

168

A third type of relationship often used in economics is *cross section* analysis. In its simplest terms, we compare the distribution of a certain economic variable among a cross section of our society. Let us take, for example, our original problem of the relationship between sale taxes and expenditure but instead of looking at Mr. Machinist at various levels of expenditure or over time, let us look at Mr. Machinist, Mr. Plumber, Mr. Doctor, Mrs. Teacher, Miss Clerk, Mr. Orderly and Miss Retired — a cross section of our society. We might get the following results.

	Purchases	Sales tax
Mr. Machinist	2,000	100
Mr. Plumber	2,600	125
Mr. Doctor	7,000	350
Mrs. Teacher	2,600	130
Miss Clerk	1,500	75
Mr. Orderly	1,800	90
Miss Retired	1,000	50

A plot of the variables of sales tax against purchases will give the same relationship that we got from the behaviour plot for Mr. Machinist in our first example.

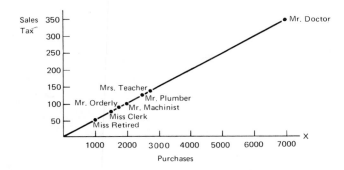

FIGURE A-5

As one can see, the graph is merely a means by which we can see at a glance how various economic values are related to each other. In general, we have placed the independent variable on the horizontal axis, the dependent variable on the vertical.

There is one major exception in economics to this rule of placing the independent variable on the X axis. This is the supply and demand graph. In this case we are picturing how quantities supplied and demanded depend on price. But for historical reasons, we put the independent variable, price, on the Y axis; the dependent variable, quantities, on the X axis. So much for the scientific consistency of economists!

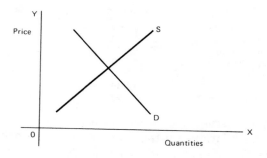

FIGURE A-6

Glossary

Aggregate Demand — The total value of goods and services demanded in an economy.

Aggregate Demand Function — The schedule of the total value of goods and services demanded at various levels of national income. $AD = C + I_{intended} + G + (X - M)$.

Aggregate Supply — The total value of goods and services supplied in an economy.

Aggregate Supply Function — The schedule of the total value of goods and services supplied at various levels of national income. $AS = C + S + T$.

Appreciation — The increase in the value of a floating currency in the world market.

Automatic Stabilizers — Those government programs that tend to increase (decrease) expenditures or decrease (increase) taxes in periods of declining (rising) national income without any change in government policy.

Autonomous Consumption — The level of consumption demand independent of the level of national income (i.e., where NNP = 0).

Autonomous Investment — The level of investment demand, independent of the level of national income (i.e., where NNP = 0).

Autonomous Savings — The level of savings independent of the level of national income (i.e., where NNP = 0).

Availability of Credit Doctrine — The concept that credit is rationed, not by the pricing of credit (i.e., by the interest rate), but by some institutional allocation mechanism.

Average Propensity to Consume — The ratio of consumption demand to national income at any given level of national income. $APC = \dfrac{C}{Y}$.

Average Propensity to Save — The ratio of savings to national income at any given level of national income. $APS = \dfrac{S}{Y}$.

Balance of Payments — The accounts of a country's receipts from and payments to the rest of the world.

Balance of Trade — The accounts of a country's receipts from its commodity exports to and payments for commodity imports from the rest of the world.

Bank Rate — The interest rate charged by the Bank of Canada on loans to the chartered banks and to certain money market dealers; acts as a signal to the economy of central bank monetary policy.

Bonds — Promisary notes of fixed face value and date of maturity, usually bearing a designated interest rate or interest payment.

Capital — Produced goods (buildings, equipment and machinery, inventory) used, not for themselves, but for the production of other goods.

Capital Consumption Allowances — Savings set aside by businesses to provide for the depreciation, or using up, of capital.

Cash Drain — The cash (currency and coin) that is withdrawn by the public for transaction purposes out of any new deposit money created by the banking system.

Cash Reserve — The assets in cash (currency and coin) and deposits in the central bank held by financial intermediaries against their deposit liabilities.

Cash Reserve — The ratio the chartered banks are required by law to hold of assets in the form of cash reserve to deposits.

Ceteris Paribus — A Latin expression meaning "Other things remaining the same".

Chartered Banks — Federally incorporated and regulated financial intermediaries whose demand and savings deposits constitute the predominant portion of the Canadian money supply.

Commercial Policy — Policy relating to the international segment of aggregate demand, including exchange rate and tariff policies.

Comparative Advantage — The advantage in the international competitive position of a country due to its greater relative efficiency in the production of a certain good or service.

Comprehensive Theory — A theory containing a large number of explanatory variables; the larger the number of variables, the more comprehensive the theory.

Consumer Price Index (CPI) — An index of the average prices of a certain basket of consumer goods (selected on the basis of actual consumer expenditure for an average family) related to some base year.

Consumption Function — The schedule of the value of consumption expenditure at various levels of national income.

Cost Push Inflation — Inflation initiated by rising costs of production (due to autonomous increases in wages, rents, interest, profits or imported inputs) independent of the level of demand.

Currency — Paper money.

Current Account — The statement of receipts from and payments to the rest of the world for exports and imports of goods and services.

Capital Account — The statement of receipts from and payments to the rest of the world of loans, either in the form of long run loans or short term loans.

Deflationary Gap — The excess of aggregate supply over aggregate demand at full employment.

Demand Deposits — Deposits in financial intermediaries which are payable on demand, usually non- or low-interest bearing.

Demand Pull Inflation — Inflation initiated by an excess of aggregate demand for goods and services over the available aggregate supply of goods and services at full employment.

Depreciation — (1) The decrease in the value of a floating currency in the world market; (2) The decline in the value of capital stock due to it being "used up" in the production of other goods or services.

Depression — A cyclical down swing in the economy producing unemployment and a level of economic activity well below potential. Small depressions are frequently called recessions.

Elasticity of Investment — A measure of the responsiveness of the quantity of investment to changes in the interest rate.

Equilibrium — The state reached when a system comes to rest, and from which no movement will take place unless one or more of the balancing forces is altered.

Exchange Rate — the rate at which one country's money can be traded for the money of another country.

Ex Ante — Before the fact; *ex ante* savings and investment means intended savings and investment over some future period.

Ex Post — After the fact; *ex post* savings and investment means realized savings and investment over some past period.

Factors — Inputs into production; composed of land labour and capital.

Financial Intermediaries — Institutions in the money market which collect the savings of one sector of the economy and provide credit for the borrowing sector.

Fiscal Policy — Policy relating to the government sector of national income and expenditure, including tax, transfer payments and government expenditure policies.

Fixed (or Pegged) Exchange Rate — An exchange rate of one nation's currency set by government action at some fixed value in terms of another currency or of gold. Fixed rates are normally allowed to fluctuate in value within a very narrow range.

Flexible (or floating) Exchange Rate — The exchange rate of a nation's currency determined freely by the supply and demand for that currency in world exchange markets.

Foreign Exchange Fund — A fund of foreign currency reserves and gold managed by the government and central bank for purposes of stabilizing the exchange rate at its pegged value in the case of a fixed rate, or ironing out minor day to day fluctuations in value in the case of a flexible rate.

Full Employment — (1) In Keynesian theoretical terms, that rate of employment where all available factors are in use and no increase in real output can be obtained through increased aggregate demand; (2) in practical policy terms, a low rate of unemployment (approximately 3%) where, because of structural imbalances and frictions in the economy, increases in real output through increased aggregate demand can only be achieved at the expense of unacceptably high levels of inflation.

General Agreement on Tariffs and Trade (GATT) — An agreement begun in 1948 and covering approximately 70 countries designed to facilitate the reduction of barriers to trade, and the removal of quantity import controls and the reduction of tariffs.

General Equilibrium — Equilibrium in a general system of equations; the simultaneous solution for all of the variables in a general theory.

General Theory — A theory in which all of the variables included are completely and simultaneously determined.

Gross Investment — Total expenditure in a given period on capital goods and inventory, including expenditure for the replacement of capital goods used up in the period (depreciation).

Gross National Expenditure — The market value of the total expenditure of all sectors of the economy, including the net foreign sector, on final goods and services.

Gross National Product — The value of the total stream of income payments to factors, indirect tax payments to governments, and savings allocated to offset depreciation; equal to the value of total production.

Gross Domestic Product — Income originating in Canada. Differs from GNP by excluding indirect taxes and payments to Canadians by foreigners, but including payments by Canadians to foreigners.

Gross Savings — Total income saved by firms, individuals and the government, including savings allocated for the replacement of depreciated capital goods (capital consumption allowances).

Indirect Taxes — Taxes paid by firms directly to the government before firm revenue is distributed as factor incomes.

Inflation — A general rise in the average price level.

Inflationary gap — The excess of aggregate demand over aggregate supply at full employment.

Intended Investment — Expenditure planned by investors for the following period.

Intended Savings — Savings planned by individuals, firms and the government for the following period.

International Monetary Fund (IMF) — An international monetary agency established in 1944 to facilitate the free exchange of international currencies, by the establishment of a pegged rate system and the provision of a reserve fund from which countries may borrow reserves to overcome temporary balance of payments disequilibrium.

Inventory — The stock of finished or intermediate goods produced in a given period but not sold to the final purchasers.

Liquidity — A measure of the ease with which assets may be converted into purchasing power (or money) with minimum capital loss.

Liquidity Ratio — The ratio of chartered bank assets which must be held in very liquid assets (treasury bills and day loans to money market dealers).

Liquidity Trap — The condition where the interest rate has fallen to such a level that almost everybody prefers to hold money rather than other assets yielding such low interest rates.

Long Run — The market period when all factors are variable.

174

Marginal Propensity to Consume — The ratio of the resultant change in aggregate saving to any given change in national income.

Marginal Propensity to Import — The ratio of the resultant change in imports to any given change in national income.

Marginal Propensity to Save — The ratio of the resultant change in aggregate saving to any given change in national income.

Marginal Propensity to Tax — The ratio of the change in net taxes to any given change in national income.

Macroeconomics — The study of the aggregate flows and levels of economic activity in the economy.

Microeconomics — A study of the economic processes of the constituent markets and sectors of the total economy, all other things remaining equal.

Monetary Policy — The policy of the central bank (and/or government) related to the supply of money and the level and structure of interest rates.

Money — Anything that acts as money, i.e., acts as a medium of exchange, a standard of value measurement, a store of value and a speculative asset.

Money Market — That market in which a group of institutions buy and sell financial assets (loans) making available the savings of one sector of the economy to another sector for purposes of financing investment or other expenditure.

Money Multiplier — The number of times any change in the cash reserve of the banking system is multiplied to produce the change in the money supply. Equal to $\dfrac{1}{\text{cash reserve ratio}}$.

Money Supply — In Canada, commonly considered to include currency and coin outside of the banks, demand deposits and savings deposits in the chartered banks.

Moral Suasion — A tool of monetary policy used by the Bank of Canada; consisting of persuasion by the central bank of the chartered banks, and more rarely, other financial intermediaries, to adopt some specified course of action.

Multiplier — That multiple by which national income is changed due to an autonomous change in expenditure.

Near Money — Highly liquid financial assets which, unlike money can not command directly goods and services, but which can be converted readily and at low cost or capital risk into money.

Net National Income — The value of national product actually available to factors; excludes out of gross national product only depreciation and indirect taxes.

Net National Product — The value of the total production of a national economy after allowance has been made for depreciation.

Non-Bank Financial Intermediaries — Institutions which, like the banks act as intermediaries between lenders and borrowers in the money market, but which lack the statutory right to create money, and whose liabilities do not circulate as money.

Open Market Operations — Activities by the central bank in the money market buying and selling financial assets (bonds and bills) thereby affecting the interest rates in the market and the money supply.

Partial Equilibrium — The equilibrium established in a system where one or more of the independent variables has its value determined somewhere outside the system.

Partial Theory — A theory in which the level of one or more of the explanatory variables is taken as a given, determined by a process not included in the theory.

Personal Disposable Income — That portion of national income at the discretionary disposal of individuals; excludes personal taxation.

Personal Income — That portion of national income that accrues to individuals, including government transfer payments but excluding corporate savings and taxes.

Precautionary Demand for Money — That demand for money as insurance against unexpected expenditure due to an uncertain future (closely related to transaction demand).

Quantity Theory of Money — A theory which may take several forms, but which is based on the relationship $MV = PT$, where M is the supply of money, V is the velocity of money, P is the aggregate price level, and T, the aggregate volume of goods and services produced in the economy. This relationship becomes a theory rather than a definition when we make some assumptions about the behaviour of a variable such as V in order to predict the value of one of the other variables.

Real Income — The value of income adjusted for any change in the purchasing power of that income due to changes in prices.

Realized Investment — Investment expenditure actually achieved in some given time period.

Realized Savings — Savings actually achieved in some given time period.

Revaluation — The official raising of the value of a currency on a pegged exchange rate.

Short run — The market period when at least one factor is fixed.

Speculative Demand for Money — That demand for money in order to speculate on changes in the interest rate on other financial assets.

Stable Equilibrium — An equilibrium to which a system tends to return if disturbed from that initial position.

Stabilization — Policies designed to reduce fluctuations in some economic variable, bringing the economy to a stable equilibrium at or near full employment without inflation.

Stocks — Financial assets of no specified face value or term which normally involve some ownership equity and which are valued at the expected capitalized stream of dividends.

Tariff — A tax levied on imports.

Trade-Off — The concept that full employment can only be achieved at some rate of price increase and that price stability can only be achieved at some rate of unemployment, necessitating some compromise on the dual goals of full employment and price stability.

Treasury Bills — A particular type of government bond of either 91 or 181 days maturity having a quoted face value but no interest rate, the rate being determined by the difference between face value and market value.

Transaction Demand for Money — The demand for money for purposes of carrying out normal payments and purchases; related to the level of national income but not normally to the interest rate.

Value Added — The contribution to gross national product of a specific firm or stage of production; excludes the value of previous non-factor inputs, i.e., selling price less cost of raw materials, intermediate goods, etc.

Velocity of Money — The average number of times a unit of money is spent per period of time; i.e., total expenditure per year ÷ supply of money.

Index